Teach Me, Mummy!

Developmental exercises from birth to school age

Published 2011 by Dean & Co. Publishing Ltd. Ireland
Text and illustrations copyright © 2011 Dean & Co. Publishing Ltd.

Typesetting, layout and design: SOS System

Printed in the EU

ISBN 978-1-908112-01-9

Edited by Síne Quinn

Proofread by Natasha Mac a'Bháird

www.deanandcopublishing.com
www.awareparents.com
Email: info@deanandcopublishing.com

Kathy Dean

Teach Me, Mummy!

Developmental exercises from birth to school age

Aware PARENTS

Acknowledgements

Publisher's acknowledgement

I have had the pleasure of knowing and observing Kathy Dean's educational work over many years. I witnessed how she taught her pupils with enthusiasm, patience and affection both in a group environment and in a one-to-one set up. Kathy developed the Aware Parents programme by building on this experience. Her educational methods have been tested and piloted by many parents and teachers in training, all with great success. Some say it marks the beginning of an era. Thank you to all who participated in the process of publishing this book. Please read this book with trust, goodwill and love – the same way it was written.

Table of contents

Preface

American and Japanese research results have clearly proven that children who receive systematic and specific early education from their parents or carers have a significantly higher intelligence, better learning skills and stronger self confidence than those left alone during their early years to explore the world themselves.

This book is designed to help and support parents and carers who feel that a child's development is important from the beginning. It provides activities which will stimulate a child mentally, physically and emotionally. The programme is designed to improve verbal skills, language development, physical agility, hand-eye coordination, observation and motor skills, all of which are important in a child's early education.

This programme offers a simple day-to-day activity list that is clearly laid out with lots of fun activities which both adult and young child will enjoy.

These joint activities will help parents gradually gain an insight into the likes and dislikes, strengths and weaknesses of their child. The activities will encourage the adult to support the child in their overall developmental process.

Guidelines for the programme

This learning programme is designed to start at a very young stage, just when the baby reaches the 2-3 week old mark. By this time the parent and baby bond has started to become stronger, and there is an established daily routine.

During the first few months, the learning sessions should be timed for when the baby is awake and alert. Never wake up the child for the sake of a session. An ideal time is when they have just had their nappy changed, they have been fed and they are comfortable. Later you can pick a suitable time when the baby is awake and you are both relaxed. When the baby is 4-5 months, the ideal playtime should be scheduled for the same time every day, for example, every afternoon.

At first the sessions should last only a few minutes, becoming longer as the months go by. It is very important to be patient and calm when doing the sessions. Never tell the child off or get annoyed if she is unsuccessful in a task. It is important that she enjoys the sessions and feels comfortable. Encourage and praise her success with a big kiss or applause and later with compliments. Remember to celebrate success together – it is advisable to only show her achievement to her immediate family circle.

When the child is tired or sick do not force tasks on them. If the child gets upset or cranky or becomes distracted stop the task or activity. The activities that the child cannot complete should be marked in a notebook and repeated at a later stage. If you miss a few weeks of the programme, mark it and get back to it later. It is worth indicating if the task turned out to be enjoyable for the child, so that they can enjoy it again when repeating it.

Sometimes, after starting an activity the child might take it in her own direction, leading it away from the designed task. If this happens do not force the planned task, but rather, support her in her unfolding idea and see where it leads.

Keep the book in a handy place, so that you can read it at any time. Keeping a notebook is also a useful way to trace the development and the success of the sessions. The programme is neither strict nor rigid. It is okay if you miss a few days. The main point of the programme is for the child to enjoy learning and trying new activities.

I am not suggesting a specific programme for the first few months (0-4).

Take your pick from the list of activities every day. From the 4th month onwards until the age of 14 months, every two months you are going to get a day-to-day list of activities. From this age on you will find ten day-to-day session plans for each month. These session plans are tailored to the child's monthly development.

Study the contents page so that you can fully understand the structure of the book.

Do not lose heart if the suggested activities seem to be difficult for your child. Remember that every child develops and grows in their own time. Some children are more able for an activity earlier, some later. You will see your efforts will soon bear fruit.

I hope the ideas in my book will help you have an enjoyable time with your child while enriching her intellectual and emotional life.

I wish you success and joy, and I hope you have fun playing!

Useful tips and comments on parenting and education

- Most parents realise that parenting their child is the greatest undertaking of their life.
- From the moment of birth your child should be taught to believe that she will be successful in life.
- Learn to make sacrifices for your child.
- Love should be the ultimate guide for parenting.
- Interest should be the main motivation for education.
- Internal values should have priority over external values.
- Most of your spare time should be spent on doing things with your child.
- You should accept that your child is different from you, and celebrate the difference.

- Show a good example.
- Never say: 'You are too young to understand'.
- Be flexible but consistent.
- Always believe in what your child says.
- Do not try to force things if she is not ready for it.
- Do not teach anything that is only good for you to boast about.
- Always notice your child's good qualities.
- Work out a strategy to overcome any bad characteristics.
- Let your child communicate with people outside of the family.
- Give support to your child in expressing disagreement. Although she wants to, a child might be too young to argue.
- Do not compare your child to other children.
- Give respect to your child, she is a person too.
- Be happy that destiny gave you the chance to fulfil a miracle by bringing up your child.

Activity images used for the first 36 months

Congratulations on the birth of your baby. The first three months of a child's life are exciting for both the parents and the child. The following activities are ways which will help encourage bonding, communication and awareness in a fun and relaxed way. Enjoy the activities and remember every child is different and each one develops and advances in their own way.

This section concentrates on the following exercises and developments

 Exercises for developing bodily awareness and motion skills

 Tactile information and exercises for developing fine motor skills

 Exercises for developing sight

 Auditory information

 Activities aimed at enriching the baby's emotional wellbeing

 Recommendations for developing independent play

 Games for exploring the environment

 Ideas for developing mimicking skills

 Speech development exercises

 Activities for developing intellectual skills and providing factual information

Developmental activities for the 1st month

During the first few months of life sensual information plays the main role in education. The newborn baby's life is controlled by unconditioned reflexes. These are innate life functions, which enable the child to breathe, feed and get rid of waste material.

Learning, starting off with information being delivered by the senses, will become possible through a number of conditioned reflex chains. At an early stage the main thing will be to set these chains of reflexes in motion.

Naturally, the baby's mood must be taken into consideration before beginning any of the activities. The most important thing is to ensure that the child adapts to her surroundings. That she is comfortable and that both baby and parent/minder are relaxed. Ensure that your baby has been fed, has a clean nappy, is not over tired or uncomfortable. (Note: if your baby shows discomfort in any way, stop immediately. You can begin to try the particular exercise again the next day.)

Bodily awareness
Tactile skills
Sight
Hearing
Emotional wellbeing

With this programme a newborn can really benefit from small things, such as changing bodily position, mastering her visual and auditory skills. She can get important information using touch, as skin has the most extensive surface of all the sense organs. The following are simple and easy ways to help your newborn develop bodily awareness, stimulate tactile skills, help to enrich her emotional wellbeing, and develop her sight and hearing:

 To develop bodily awareness
- Turn the baby onto her side (for a short period).
- Turn her onto her tummy for a few minutes.
- Rock her very gently.

 To stimulate tactile skills
- Gently caress her back, arms and legs.
- Massage these body parts in a gentle way.
- Leave her without clothes after bath time, ensuring that the temperature of the room is appropriate.
- Carefully stretch her legs, and loosen the hip by pushing the thighs apart. Do this very gently. Do not overdo it.
- Make bath time a pleasant experience by ensuring the water is the correct temperature (you can use a bath thermometer to ensure that it is the right temperature).
- Dress her in soft and comfortable clothing (and if it isn't too cold leave her uncovered for a little while). A newborn needs to learn how

to see and to focus. In the first few days of her life the eyes are not yet able to produce a perfect image.

Exercises for developing sight
• Vary the baby's position in her cot or Moses basket.
• Vary the brightness of the lighting in her room (you can use bright lights after using dim lights).
• Protect her eyes from very strong lights, such as sunshine or bright lamps.

Exercises for developing hearing
• Try to protect your baby from loud or sudden noises. This is not always easy, especially if you have other children.
• Whenever she is awake, talk to her in a kind voice.
• Sing or hum quietly to soothe her.
• Putting on some nice and quiet music in her room is a good idea, but not for longer than 15-30 minutes.

Activities aimed at enriching emotional wellbeing
• Spend some time outdoors up to 30-45 minutes, weather permitting. This can improve both you and your baby's spirit.
• Smile at her often and chat to her in a kind voice, which will give her comfort.
• Do not let visitors disturb the newborn's peace. (If she is asleep when they call, don't wake her. Let her wake on her own.)
• Do not leave her to cry. In the first few months of her life, try to calm your baby when she cries by holding her, singing to her, saying 'sssh' and rocking her or swaying her gently. Often newborn babies find comfort in being swaddled and held. Don't always offer her milk (breast or bottle) the minute she cries. She might not always be hungry and it is a good idea to find another way to comfort her without depending on milk straight away. This is the corner stone of building trust. In time you will be able to identify her different cries and know if she is hungry, tired, needs her nappy changed or just needs to be held.

Developmental activities up to 3 months of age

By one month and over a baby is already communicating in his or her own way, and is eager to communicate more. The baby might even be smiling. Family life might be easier now, and things have probably started to settle down once everyone has got used to having a newborn in the house. You might have managed to form a daily routine, and have more of an idea when your baby is awake and what times she naps.

Bodily awareness
Sight
Hearing
Emotional wellbeing
Independent play

During the alert periods the baby is showing more of an interest in the world around her. Watch out for her gestures and signs of alertness when you are doing the activities.

 Exercises to develop bodily awareness
- Continue doing everything that was suggested for the previous month (massage, turning the baby onto her tummy and her side). In addition, you can do some exercises with her. The ideal time for this is after the baby's bath. Make sure the temperature is appropriate then do these movements with the undressed baby. Firstly, repeat them once or twice, then later, two or three times – only if she likes doing them.
- From a lying position pull the baby's arms up next to her head, then down next to the sides of her body.
- Still having her lying on her back, bend her knees carefully, push her thighs against her tummy, open the thighs, and then, after having loosened her hips, stretch both legs. (Note: Do these exercises very gently! Do not do any of these exercises if your baby was breech, or has any hip, leg or back problems!)
- Lay her on her tummy, and then gently slide two fingers along her spine a few times.
- Lay her naked on your own or her daddy's naked chest.
- Caress certain points of her body to soothe her, for instance, nose, eyebrows, double chin, ears. Try to find out which her favourite area is.

 Exercises to develop sight
Lay the baby on her tummy in her cot, making sure she can see out in more than one direction.
- Hang a big piece of colourful material with big patterns (shawl, tablecloth, etc.) on the side of the cot (remember to remove it after the exercise).
- The cot undersheets can have patterns on them, too. (Any kind of bedding cover will do as a cot sheet.)

- Hang sparkling objects on the side of the cot, for example, a paper Christmas tree decoration.
- Tie colourful and sparkling objects on the cot in such a way that they hang above the baby.
- Try to catch her attention by showing her a toy and encourage her to follow it sideways and upwards with her eyes.
- Move the baby's hand in her view, so that she notices it, and then move it sideways.
- Close her hands in front of her eyes then open them up again.
- Put a light object in the baby's hand and try to ensure that she focuses on it a few times.
- Carry the baby to the window then walk with her to darker parts of the house and then back to the light again, slowly. Observe her reaction.

The practice of handling objects helps to develop hand-eye coordination. Activities that promote the development of links between these two senses (touch and sight) are important.

Exercises for developing hearing
- Talk to your baby even when she cannot see you.
- Whatever you are doing around the baby, talk to her in a friendly way.
- Play peek-a-boo. Appear from various parts of the cot and say: 'Peek-a-boo!' Do not frighten her!
- You can play music in her room for half an hour to one hour (this length of time adds up from a few 15-20 minute long periods).
- Try to get her attention by using a rattle. She will respond to the various sources of sound by turning her head.

Activities aimed at enriching emotional wellbeing
- Gradually increase the length of time spent outdoors.
- Take your time when giving her a bath – let her enjoy it.
- Smile at her often.
- Imitate her utterances, and copy her vocalisations (purring, gargling, baby talk).

Independent play

Between the 1st and 3rd months there will come a time when the baby does not fall asleep immediately after feeding. If she is left alone and nothing is happening to her, she will easily get upset and try to call her playmate back by crying. If this happens it is enough that the parent stands by her cot and talks to her to make her feel better. Now is a good time to encourage her to start to have some independent play time. A way to begin this process is to try and engage her in paying attention to the objects around her, even if for a short while. Otherwise she will not let you have a moment to yourself later. Independent play helps to develop concentration. Later, when the child is older, independent play is a good time for the child to begin to use their imagination and take the time to play by themselves. It can also be relaxing for a child because it allows them to get lost in play and not depend on outside stimulus to entertain them. Independent play needs to be encouraged systematically and consistently to your baby. Below are some ideas to get you and your baby started:

- Stretch a ribbon over the cot and hang colourful mobile figures or rattles on it (ensure they are tied securely and are safe). Before leaving the baby alone, direct her attention to these toys. Her peaceful play must not be disturbed either by you or somebody else.
- Turn the baby onto her side and place a plastic animal or a colourful teething toy within her reach near her hands. (If she gets bored with this, try out new positions.)
- Turn her onto her tummy and place the toys further away from her, so that she can see but cannot reach them.
- Take the baby to a different room, put her down on her back on a play mat or a comfortable rug, leave her alone and let her look around (ensure that she is in a safe location and is content).
- Hang an easily detachable bright picture next to her cot.
- Do not cram all her toys in her cot – place only one or two in the cot.
- Her independent play is very important, especially as her alert periods will become longer and longer and it will be very hard for you to entertain her all the time. The more she plays independently, the more she will enjoy it. It is important to ensure that she is comfortable and that she does not need anything before you start. Try not to pick her up when she whimpers or is bored, instead try another suggested activity and see if she will respond to it before picking her up.

Gradually encourage your baby to play independently.

Developmental activities from 4 months up to sitting up (4-7 months of age)

Babies vary in terms of when they learn to turn, crawl or sit up. Each baby develops at his or her own pace; there is no point comparing your baby's development to other babies' the same age. Over time, infants with a healthy development become more and more skilled in their movements. The amount of change that they go through during this period of their life is unbelievable. Enjoy this time with your child and celebrate the progression you see in them. It is important to continue the learning activities. The time for play can be increased gradually: 15-30 minutes per day allows you both to learn a lot. Use a blanket or the couch for the sessions rather than her cot. Ensure that the surface is safe and you are both comfortable before beginning. (Try to do the activities every day at the same time. If you miss a day, don't worry you can always return to them the following day.)

A few safety tips for this period
• Do not leave the baby unattended on any elevated surface.
• If she has started experimenting with crawling, remove all potentially dangerous objects off the floor.
• Avoid using low hanging tablecloths that the baby can reach and pull down.
• Apply socket covers and fit safety latches to cabinets, drawers and presses.
• Dangerous areas (fireplaces, glass cabinets, plant stands, unstable shelves, stairs) should be blocked by using safety gates, chairs or other obstacles.

Activities aimed at developing the child's intellectual abilities, attention and thinking step in as part of the programme during this age period, and they will become more and more emphasised as time goes by. Supporting development at this stage mainly means developing the senses through play. At this stage you will be able to observe the results of the sessions. You might notice that your baby is much more relaxed and balanced and is more content. You will notice that shared activities also become a basis for independent play. A child who is occupied and supported in her development in a complex manner is less likely to become bored, whiny or whinge. Here are some more ideas for joint activities:

Exercises aimed at developing tactile information

- Acquaint the child with various materials she can touch. Put a piece of silk, a piece of cotton, and a sample of roughly woven linen in her hand. Stroke her small hands with these materials and observe her reaction. Tickle her hands and face with a feather.
- Put a soft ball, a rag doll and then a hard object (a spoon or a building block) in her hand.
- Put a soft toy in one of her hands, and a hard toy in the other. Watch what she does.
- Show her objects that are interesting to touch (a plaster, a piece of paper, some tin foil, a sponge).
- Roll a small ball in her hand so that she can feel the smooth, round surface.
- Roll an angular object in her hand, and then draw her tiny hand along the edges.
- Show her how to bang the table with the different objects she has and let her bang away.
- Lay the baby naked on a soft blanket, and then lay her on a couch with a rough surface.
- Gently scratch her back, tummy, hands and legs.
- Kiss different parts of her skin, for instance, her back, tummy, hands and feet. Do not tickle her as this can mean too much stimulation for the baby.
- Using her hand stroke the baby's head and hair.
- While you are doing these activities talk to her and explain what you are doing. Use the words to describe the different sensations: soft, rough, smooth, silky, hard, heavy and light.

Exercises for developing sight

- Put a colourful object in her hand and move it so that it is in front of her eyes.
- Move the baby's arm, and try to persuade her to follow it with her eyes.
- Hang a toy up in her cot in such a way that she can reach it and bang it.
- Hang a bright, patterned tablecloth up the side of her cot.
- Attach light, colourful paper cut-outs (fish, birds), which can be moved easily by any movement of air, on the ceiling light.
- Put a toy in front of her and encourage her to take it.
- Giving her objects of different sizes, try to teach her how to hold objects with one hand and then with both hands.

Exercises to develop hearing

• Using a rattle, draw her attention to different directions.
• Play with a whistling plastic toy.
• Knock plastic, wooden and metal toys against one another in front of her. Then put these objects in her hand and help her do the knocking.
• If you can afford it, get her a musical toy that plays a nice, calming melody.
• Sing to her daily.
• Listen to music and conversations on the radio. (Remember: if the radio is on all day you cannot use it for directing the child's attention.)
• Draw her attention to various sounds, for example: 'Listen to the car!' or 'Can you hear it? Listen, it's a dog barking!'
• Show her one by one what noise the household appliances make (vacuum cleaner, washing machine, blender, etc.). If she gets frightened or seems to be afraid turn the machine off and reassure her.

Activities aimed at enriching emotional wellbeing

Follow the suggested activities in the 1-3 months chapter. Shared, carefree play enriches the bond and emotional wellbeing of both parent and child.

Here's a list of suggested activities for both of you to enjoy:
• Both of you lie down facing each other on your side.
• Make faces and try to make the baby laugh.
• Continue making faces and stick out your tongue. See if the baby copies you, and if she does encourage her to continue.
• Stick your finger in the baby's mouth so that she bites it then wail and laugh. (Wash your hands before the game!)
• Put a shawl or blanket in her hand. Pretend that you're trying to take it away from her. This 'rope pulling' is great fun.
• Play wrestling. Snuggle up to each other and try to gently chew on her tiny hands and feet.
• Make a happy face, then a serious one. Watch her reaction and see if she copies you. Clap your hands and then clap her tiny hands together.
• Play on her fingers: 'This little piggy went to market, this little piggy stayed at home. This little piggy had roast beef. And this little piggy had none. This little piggy went wee, wee, wee, all the way home.'
• Play: 'Round and round the garden, like a teddy bear, one step, two step, tickle you under there!'
• Play: 'Row, row, row your boat, Gently down the stream, Merrily, merrily, merrily, merrily, Life is but a dream.' Try another version of this song: 'Row, row, row your boat, Gently down the stream, If you

see a crocodile, Don't forget to scream' and then let out a little scream. Watch her laugh and see if she will also scream.
• Dance to music together.
• After each play-fight relax by cuddling up gently together. Cuddle and hug her and hum a calming melody to her.

Activities for exploring the environment
• Put the baby on a blanket on the floor in various rooms of the house.
• If the weather is good, play outside on a blanket.
• Look into a mirror together. Smile at her and see if she will smile too. Try to touch the mirror together and encourage her to reach out to the mirror.
• Pull her up into a sitting position, but do not insist on letting her sit unaided.
• Take her to other people's houses, but make sure you do not leave her under a child's supervision.
• Squash a leaf in your hand when outdoors so that she hears the sound it makes.
• Place a small fruit in her hand.
• Knock two stones against each other.
• Let her splash her bathwater.

Activities for aiding the development of mimicking skills
Objective: to persuade the baby to copy your action. This is not an easy task so don't worry if you cannot succeed from one day to the other, especially at the beginning. It might take a while for your baby to realise what you are encouraging her to do. When doing the activities, ask your baby to do the same as you, for instance: 'You smile too!'
• Smile, then make a serious face.
• Stick your tongue out, move it around, and then pull it back in.
• Turn your head sideways, then look into her face and say: 'Boo.' (Be careful not to frighten her.)
• Make her copy sounds, for example, 'g' or 'r'! Try more difficult ones: 'eh', 'ah', 'uk'!
• Make a buzzing noise for her.
• Smack your lips towards her.
• Make a surprised face.
• Blow a kiss to her.

Development of independent play

A 4-5 month old child spends more and more time being awake. It is getting increasingly difficult to fill all this time with play activities. Independent play should be introduced as part of the daily routine, either in the morning or in the afternoon. During these times let her gain experiences through her own investigations:

Take her out of the cot and put her in a playpen or on a slim mattress or blanket on the floor.
Ensure she is in a safe location away from any harmful objects or potential danger.

Place new objects around her. You don't need too many of them, just one or two. Make absolutely sure that the baby cannot swallow any of them or that she cannot hurt herself or cause an accident with them.
The objects can be toys but they can also be interesting things from around the house. You can show her an empty plastic container (put a smaller object inside the see-through version to create a great toy).
Any object that isn't a danger to her can provide a child with useful pieces of information. With the help of these new objects she can get familiar with different qualities: cold, warm, soft, hard, rigid, mobile, etc. Keep thinking about which other objects would make good toys!

Do these activities following the day-to-day lists.

Day-to-day programme
for children aged 4-5 months

1st week

Monday	• Give her a feather, a piece of silk and a piece of paper. • Encourage her to look at the object in her hand.
Tuesday	• Give her a rag doll, a spoon and a plastic building block. • Give her an object so that she can see her hand. If she doesn't notice it show it to her.
Wednesday	• Show her objects that are interesting to the touch (a plaster, a piece of paper, some tin foil, a sponge). • Attach a toy onto her cot in such a way that she can reach it with her hands.
Thursday	• Give her a ping-pong (or any small) ball, then a block. • Put a sheet with patterns on it under her and turn her on her tummy.
Friday	• Bang the table with various objects: a ball, a building block. • Move a cot toy in front of her eyes and if she reaches for it give it to her.

2nd week

Monday	• Lie down on the carpet or rug and listen to music. • Give her a whistling plastic figure and play with it.
Tuesday	• Carry her around the house in your arms and let her touch certain things. • Sing to her. Clap her hands to the rhythm.
Wednesday	• Look into a mirror. • Play with a rattle. Shake it in different directions and see if she looks for it.
Thursday	• Say nursery rhymes and move her body to the rhythm. • Pull her up from a lying position into sitting.
Friday	• Crumple up a piece of paper. • Place a few toys on the table and let her get them.

3rd week

Monday	• Show her the vacuum cleaner. • Lay her on her back and show her how you stick out your tongue. See if she will copy you.
Tuesday	• Direct her attention using a rattle. • Take her to someone else's house.
Wednesday	• Listen to music; 'dance' to the rhythm. • Imitation: smile, and then get serious.
Thursday	• Play with a toy animal to develop her focus. (It hides then it comes back.) • Rattle a leaf when outside.
Friday	• Sing a song while you touch the ground with her feet to the rhythm. • Imitation: turn your head to the side and see if she copies your move.

4th week

Monday	• Play the imitation games: turning the head sideways, sticking out your tongue. • Sit at the table and place objects further away from her so that she has to stretch out to get them. Pull them along slowly in front of her.
Tuesday	• Look in the mirror and name your body parts. • Start doing speech exercises: gargle.
Wednesday	• Put the baby on a blanket down on the floor and play with animal toys. • Sing a song to her and clap her hands to the rhythm.
Thursday	• Imitate sounds: 'ah', 'eh', and 'uh'. • Play with a rattle to improve her attention.
Friday	• Imitate smiling and serious facial expressions. • Give her objects that are soft, hard, silky, rough.

*During the 5th month repeat those activities that
your child found a little difficult.
You may select what exercises you wish to do or else follow the same list of
activities again.*

Day-to-day programme
for children aged 6-7 months

Monday	• Give the child sweet then sour food, one after the other. • Imitate sticking out the tongue.
Tuesday	• Name parts of the face in front of the mirror. • Play: 'Pat-a-cake, pat-a-cake, baker's man'.
Wednesday	• Build a castle for your child using building blocks. • Sing songs, clap her hands to the rhythm.
Thursday	• Play with a toy car or plane; imitate the sounds they make. • Put a rice cake on the table so that she can try picking it up.
Friday	• Knock two objects together. Encourage her to try it too. • Dance with her to some music.

2nd week

Monday	• Give her soft, hard and squishy objects. • Using her hands stroke both of your faces and hair.
Tuesday	• Show her and name parts of your face: the eyes, the mouth, etc. • Play: 'Row, row, row your boat'.
Wednesday	• Play with a toy car in front of her; put it into the 'garage'. Put the car in her hand. • Sing to her.
Thursday	• Make her smell a flower. Say: 'A-tchoo!' • Build a castle for her and let her knock it down.
Friday	• Play: 'This little piggy'. • Play ball. Roll it then crawl after it.

3rd week

Monday	• At bath time show her the difference between cold and warm. • Teach 'yes-no' by asking questions, for instance: 'Is there wee in the nappy? Yes?') Show her how to nod and how to shake her head.
Tuesday	• Play the 'Peek-a-boo' game. • Teach her how to put a smaller object on top of a bigger one.
Wednesday	• Drop then pick up some toys saying: 'Up, down'. • Improve her hearing: shake a rattle and ask her where the noise was coming from.
Thursday	• Play with dolls: 'Jack and Jill went up the hill, To fetch a pail of water. Jack fell down and broke his crown, And Jill came tumbling after.' • Make sad and happy faces.
Friday	• Wave from the window: 'Bye-bye, birdie!', 'Bye-bye, doggy!' • Cover objects with a cloth and ask her to take it off.

4th week

Monday	• Build an obstacle course and try to get her to crawl through and under things. • Smack your lips and ask her to copy you.
Tuesday	• Teach her the names of the body parts by asking questions: 'Where is your head?' etc. • Play hidey. Teach her: 'Here, there' (Hide a toy behind your back then keep taking it out, varying which side it appears from).
Wednesday	• Play with pots and pans from the kitchen. • Look at picture books; tell her stories.
Thursday	• Build her various structures (a tower, a train) using blocks. • Ask questions and indicate the answer to the child by nodding or shaking your head.
Friday	• Act out a scene using animal figures. • Imitate animal sounds – 'What does the doggy say?' – 'Woof, woof!'

During the 7th month repeat those activities that your child found a little difficult. You may select what exercises you wish to do or else follow the same list of activities again.

Developmental activities from sitting up to toddlerhood (7-14 months)

Tactile skills
Sight
Thinking
Environmental knowledge
Emotional wellbeing
Mimicking skills
Speech
Independent play

Children learn how to sit up at around 6-8 months, or at least they are able to sit for a longer period of time. From this time on there is a wider range of possibilities in the area of guided learning. The sitting position frees up their hands so the child can use them to do a growing number of tasks. The development of fine motor skills can be involved in the programme from this time onwards.

Developing tactile skills
- Give the child a range of objects, each with a different quality. Ensure they are harmless even if she puts them in her mouth.
- On one occasion she should be given soft and hard objects, on another occasion flexible and rigid, another time warm and cold objects, etc.
- Sample a variety of food, each with a different taste. Choose food that she can suck or chew on alone, for example: pickles (sour), savoury roll (salty), strawberry or apricot (sweet).
- Fill cups, some with warm and some with cold water, when she is having a bath. Put the child's hand into one of them and say: 'warm'; then into another and say: 'cold'. There's no need for further explanation. Repeat this game a couple of times.
- Another bath time game: give her the empty cup and say: 'light'; then fill it with water and say: 'heavy'.
- Even if she can sit, lay her down in the bath tub and let her crawl, turn on her tummy or play in it. Never leave your baby alone in the bath, not for a moment!
- Once the child can crawl you can build her an obstacle course using chairs and a table so that she can go under them.
- Scratch or stroke certain body parts of the child, for example, back, tummy, arms, legs. Name them as well.

Development of sight and thinking
- Looking in the mirror show your child her face and the details on it.
- Sit her down in front of you and show her details of your own face: the eyes, ears, mouth, teeth, tongue and then your hair framing your face.
- Cover her eyes carefully with your hands then take the hands away and say: 'Peek-a-boo!'

- Teach her the names of some body parts: 'Where is your head, nose, mouth, leg, hand etc.?'
- Ask yes-no questions and wait for the answers: 'Are you hungry?', 'Are you sleepy?', etc. Nod your head or shake it while waiting.
- Show the child the different rooms in the house: 'Let's go to the bathroom!', 'Go to daddy in the sitting room!'
- Let her play with safe kitchenware.
- Name them: 'That's the cup!', 'Here's the spoon!'
- Let her climb stairs, while you supervise. Teach her how to come down backwards.
- Teach her the meaning of 'up' and 'down'. When a toy falls say 'down'. When you pick it up say 'up'.
- Put a rice cake in front of her on the table. Ask her to pick it up.
- Push it further away from her so it's more difficult to get it.
- Put the rice cake in a cup.
- Show her the rice cake in the cup and cover it with a cloth. Ask her: 'Where's the rice cake? Find it.'
- At the age of 9-12 months start teaching the child instructions, for instance: 'Give it to mummy', 'Put it in the cup', 'Take it out', 'Go there', 'Bring it here', etc.
- Allow her to play with found objects outside, for example, stones, sticks, sand and leaves.
- Let her play in her bathtub. Show her how to fill and tip cups.
- Put floating and sinking objects in her bath water.

Activities for exploring the environment
- Give her objects that are interesting to the touch: a plaster, some sandpaper, and the soap – when in the bath.
- Allow her to squeeze the toothpaste or ketchup out of the containers.
- Encourage her to carefully have a taste of these substances.
- Let her stroke harmless animals (with their owners' permission).
- Acquaint her with as many small creatures as you can, for example, ladybirds, snails and ants. Tell her the names of the creatures.
- Give her a leaf so that she can tear it apart. Collect other things while out walking, such as, grass, acorns and horse chestnuts.
- Get her to listen to birds singing.
- In winter, put some snow or ice in her hands.
- Give her some dry sticks and show her how to break them. Say: 'crack'!
- Allow her to eat fruit (peaches, bananas or tomatoes) on her own and do not mind the mess she's making.
- Let her touch objects she shows interest in and take them into her hands.

- Be consistent. Do not give her things if she only wants them to throw them away. Get down to her level and say: 'No. Don't throw this away'. If she does it again repeat: 'No. Don't throw this away', and remove the object from her. This will help her to learn the meaning of the word 'No'. It will also show her that you don't want her to throw the objects. Say it in a level voice that is firm; do not shout. You don't want to scare her, but you need to let her know that you do not want her to do it.

Enhancing emotional wellbeing

Take particular care with the bedtime routine. Allow the bedtime routine to be an enjoyable and winding down process. After your baby's bath, dress her and snuggle up together. Read her a bedtime story and sing her a lullaby. When she is feeling sleepy and in her cot, say good night and leave the room. Try not to let her fall asleep crying – this can be easier said than done. There are many books and techniques on ways to try and encourage your baby to settle by him or herself at bedtime. Remember to trust your instincts and have a bedtime routine that works for both you and your baby.

- Play physical games together. Wrestle, punch and 'beat' each other; have a laugh.
- Comfort her whatever the problem is. Never leave her alone with any problem, even if she is responsible for the 'accident'. Talk to her and reassure her.
- Look at picture books and tell her stories – you can invent short stories yourself but they shouldn't be sad.
- Ask the child: 'Give a cuddle to teddy/mummy/daddy.'
- Let her cuddle up to you often. Show her affection – stroke and caress her, rock and kiss her.
- If the child is strong willed be firm when dealing with her. If she has done something that you don't want her to do get down to her level and talk to her. Tell what she did was wrong and why, for instance, if she pushes or hits another child: 'Hitting is sore and it hurts. Do not hit.' If she continues to do something wrong, give her a warning. Let her know that you will stop what you are doing or take away what she is messing with or remove her from the game or the area if she continues to do it. Then if she does it again remove her from the area and put her in a safe place in a corner of a room on a chair or on a step. Make sure she is safe and watch her. Leave her there for a minute. When the minute is up remind her why she is there. 'I put you here because you were hitting. I don't want you to hit.' Then bring her back to where she was and don't mention it again. In time your child will realise what she can and cannot do. This will give her boundaries.

- Often at this age some children start to throw tantrums. This is usually because they are still too young to communicate properly. When they get frustrated or do not get what they want they might throw a tantrum. If your child does this now is the time to show her that you will not give in to her when she throws a tantrum. The best thing to do is to ignore it and move away. When she notices that she doesn't get a reaction or your attention by throwing tantrums she will soon grow out of it. Be persistent and firm on this in order to avoid any problems later on.
- Now is also a good time to start a conscious teaching regime to create limits and boundaries. Think about what things you are going to let her do and things that you think she shouldn't do, for instance, hitting or climbing on furniture. Remember to be consistent about it in order to avoid any confusion.
- Be firm but always be kind and patient to your child.

Developing mimicking skills
- Smack your lips and encourage her to copy you.
- Wave 'goodbye'.
- Play: 'Pat-a-cake, pat-a-cake'.
- Make a happy face followed by a sad one.
- Stick out your tongue.
- Using her hand stroke her hair and then your hair. Ask her to do it on her own.
- Smell a flower and say: 'A-tchoo!'
- Knock two objects against each other, and then give the objects to her and help her to do it by herself.
- Cough and say: 'Bad cough'.
- Play on her fingers or toes: 'This little piggy'.

Speech exercises

From the age of 7-8 months spend about 5-10 minutes daily on these exercises.

- During shared play push along a toy car and make engine sounds 'vroom-vroom'.
- Play with dolls: 'Jack and Jill'.
- Hide a toy then bring it back saying 'here' and 'there'.
- Wave 'bye-bye' at the window.
- Speak into a toy phone: 'Hello'.
- Give her the phone and see if she does it too.
- Look at picture books together. Name the animals or objects using one word.
- Often repeat short word pairs like 'tic-tac', 'splish-splash', and 'ding-dong'.

Independent play

This period (7-14 months) is the most important time for aiding the development of independent play. The ever-shortening sleep periods and the increasing length of time spent awake can cause major problems in those families where young children cannot engage themselves in playing on their own for half an hour to one hour a day.

I have seen young children standing in their playpen or play room, which is loaded with toys, crying and insisting that somebody plays with them, many times. In other cases the child's play period ended as soon as she finished throwing all the toys out of the playpen.

Fortunately, there is a simple way to solve this problem. If the child encounters the same toys every day she will get bored with them. After a while, none of them will catch her attention leading to frustration and boredom, resulting in her getting annoyed and either crying for attention or throwing the toys out of her playpen.

The solution: collect all the toys in the house. (Include those household items that can be used as toys!) Arrange them in groups of 4-5 items and put them in boxes or baskets. These can be referred to as 'activity packages'.

Take one of these packages every day and give it to the child, a different one each day. This way the toys will be new to the child and she will be keener on exploring and playing with them. If she still throws everything out give her only one toy. If she throws this one away as well, then say gently but firmly: 'No. I don't want you to throw the toys', then let her be bored for a little while before returning the toy.

Here are a few useful ideas on how to assemble
the contents of the boxes:

Box 1

a plastic cup, a rattling block, a textile handkerchief, a small toy car

Box 2

a plastic container with a big screw top, a small object that fits in the
container, a squeaky plastic toy, a picture book with rigid pages

Box 3

a box with a fold-up lid, a ball, a toy that can be attached to the
playpen with an elastic band, a few small objects that fit in the box

Box 4

two stackable cups, two ping-pong balls, a rattle,
small animal figures or dolls

Box 5

a reel with a small amount of thread, a plastic bowl, a sheet of
cardboard with finger size holes in (show her how to put fingers
through them and move them on the other side), a spoon, a cup

Week by week make changes to the contents of the boxes. Renew the toy
selection. Do not buy new toys – try and be creative instead.

When the child is starting independent play put music on from the radio
or a children's CD with nursery rhymes. Alternatively, you could play
some classical music. Often children enjoy listening to classical music
because it has a soothing effect on them.

Do these exercises following the day-to-day activity lists.

Day-to-day programme
for children aged 8-9 months

Monday

- Imitate animal sounds. Use a picture book or toy animals, for example, cow – moo; duck – quack-quack; cat – meow-meow.
- Give her leaves when you are outside so that she can tear them apart or crush them.

Tuesday

- Listen to music and move her on your lap to the rhythm.
- Read a book with rigid pages.

Wednesday

- Caress her with a piece of silk or linen on her arms, legs and feet.
- Sit behind the sitting child on the floor and appear from the right, then from the left, and so on. Say: 'Peek-a-boo!'

Thursday

- Teach her: 'Hickory, dickory, dock, The mouse ran up the clock. The clock struck one, The mouse ran down, Hickory, dickory, dock.'
- Give her a ping-pong or other floating balls to play with in the bath.

Friday

- Put some rice cereal or other small pieces of food in a bowl and let her nibble away.
- If the child can crawl give her a bigger toy car. Put a few things in it.

2nd week

Monday	• Arrange building blocks in a row. Give her one as well and show her where to put it. • Play with two toy animals or dolls. Pretend the dolls/toys are having a conversation about different body parts.
Tuesday	• Roll a ball. Go after it crawling and encourage her to copy you. • Show her how to pretend to cough and sneeze.
Wednesday	• Place some food further away from her on the table. Watch how she tries to get it. • Go to someone else's house so she gets used to other people.
Thursday	• Do exercises with her. Lay her on her back, bend and stretch her arms and legs. • Put a cup, a plate and a spoon in front of her. Ask her to hand them over one by one. 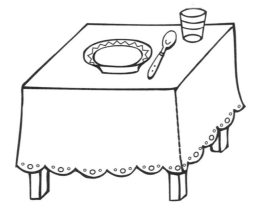
Friday	• Practise the names of the body parts. Put her hand to the appropriate part of her body, for instance, 'This is your hair, leg, hand, tummy.' • When outdoors knock two stones against each other and encourage her to do the same.

Monday
- Play a hunting game: scatter a few toys around the floor. Both of you try to reach them first crawling on the floor. Try to get ahead of the child but then let her get them before you.
- Imitate animal sounds.

Tuesday
- Put small pieces of food on a plate and let her eat with her hands (ensure you stay with her and watch her while she eats).
- Give her a shawl or scarf and play 'rope-pulling'.

Wednesday
- Sit her in a big toy car or a box and pull her around.
- Say nursery rhymes, for example, 'Incy Wincy spider, Climbed up the water spout; Down came the rain, And washed poor Incy out; Out came the sun, And dried up all the rain; And the Incy Wincy spider, Climbed up the spout again.'

Thursday
- Give her a cloth napkin in her bath. Show her the dripping water when you take it out of the water.
- Let her play in a sandbox. Give her a shovel. Help her fill a container or a bucket with sand.

Friday
- Give her a sheet of paper so she can tear it to pieces or crumple it up. Pick up the pieces. Ask her to put them in your hand.
- Build a castle in front of her using a few blocks.

4th week

Monday	• Balance a small empty box on top of the sitting child's head and watch her reaction. • Try to stack objects, for example, 3 plastic cups.
Tuesday	• Show her a plastic container with a screw top. • Crawl along an obstacle course (use chairs to narrow the lane).
Wednesday	• Recite a nursery rhyme. Clap her hands together to the beat, 'Baa-baa black sheep'. • Do exercises. Lay her on her back and lift her arms and legs. Now lay her on her side and do the same.
Thursday	• Act out a short scene using toy animals (make them talk about what they have just eaten). • Put a stick through hoops of different sizes.
Friday	• Play: 'This little piggy'. • Play the mirror game: sit down facing each other and nod your head, move your upper body, stick your tongue out.

During the 9th month you can repeat the activities your child found a little difficult. You can assemble the programme yourself or follow the list of activities in the book again.

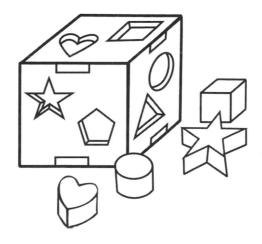

Daily activities for children aged 10-11 months

Monday	• Sit the child on the floor by an open door on the inside. Play peek-a-boo (ensure she can't get her fingers stuck in the door). • Listen to the clock ticking. Imitate the sound and move to the beat.
Tuesday	• Do exercises with her first on her back, then on her tummy. • Look at a book or a newspaper/magazine.
Wednesday	• Hold the child under her arms and swing her to the beat of the following rhyme: 'Bye, baby Bunting, Daddy's gone a hunting, To get a little rabbit skin, To wrap his baby Bunting in.' • Look at a picture book. Name objects and living things by using only one word while pointing at the picture, for example, 'dog'.
Thursday	• Look in the mirror and name your body parts, for example, 'Show me your head!' • Play with a bigger toy car. Put things into it, push it along and make engine sounds.
Friday	• Tie a toy onto the child's cot using an elastic band so she can play pulling (stay with her to ensure it is safe and remove it when the activity is over). • Pretend to cough and sneeze; encourage her to do the same.

2nd week

Monday	• Put small crackers/rice cakes in a cup and show her how to pour them out into a bowl. Practise more. Break the crackers/rice cakes. • Play with putting objects into other objects.
Tuesday	• Put a plastic bowl in front of her with some crackers/rice cakes inside. Cover it. • Listen to music. Squeeze her gently and dance.
Wednesday	• Build structures using building blocks. • Say a nursery rhyme and clap your hands to the beat: 'Dance little baby, dance up high, Never mind, baby, mother is by; Crow and caper, caper and crow, There, little baby, there you go.
Thursday	• Place a book or a newspaper on the child's head so that she balances it. • Play rolling a ball and hunting for it. Crawl on the floor.
Friday	• At lunchtime give her a spoon and let her try to use it on her own. • Switch the light on and off and teach her: dark – bright.

3rd week

Monday	• Play with puppets (the topic of your play: illness, going to the doctor). • Practise the meaning of cold and warm at bath time.
Tuesday	• Tap two stones together when outside. Put them in a small bucket. Let her lift and feel the weight. • Allow her to play with harmless kitchen equipment. Name the objects.
Wednesday	• Place a book or a pillow on the child's head to balance. • Give her food then ask her to give you some of it, too.
Thursday	• Pull at a scarf and wrestle a bit. • Practise smacking your lips and waving goodbye.
Friday	• Sing her short songs. • Put a biscuit or finger biscuit in one of her hands and a pickled gherkin in the other. When she has a taste say: sweet – sour.

Monday	• Tie a piece of string on a toy, put the end of the string inside her cot and leave the toy outside. If she doesn't do anything show her how to get the toy by pulling the string. • Build a tunnel big enough for a toy car to go under it. Show your child how to push the car through in a way that the tunnel doesn't fall down. Let her practise it again and again.
Tuesday	• Do some hand and foot exercises. Put the child on your lap, hold her hands and let her lean back so that she sees the world upside down – for a couple of seconds. Hold her under the arms and have a spin around. • Look at a book and ask her about the objects in the pictures. Ask her questions: 'Where's the table?'
Wednesday	• Visit friends and let your child play with the different toys. • Practise naming body parts. She should know where her head, hair, hands, feet and tummy are.
Thursday	• Make her go through obstacles and narrow the lanes. See whether she looks for alternative routes. • Looking at a book talk about who is doing what.
Friday	• Practise instructions: 'Bring it here', 'Give it to me', 'Put it in'. • Copy each other. Sit and fall down, raise your arms high up, lower your head down. Play peek-a-boo.

During the 11th month repeat the activities your child found a little difficult. You can either assemble the programme yourself or you can follow the list in the book.

Daily activities for children aged 12-13 months

Monday	• Look at pictures in a storybook together. You can point at a detail and name it. Do this with a few pictures. • Hold your child's hands and clap to the rhythm of a nursery rhyme or children's song.
Tuesday	• Pretend to be in a tent. Cover yourselves with a sheet or a light blanket. You can lift it with your leg slowly a couple of times. • When out walking, show your child the clouds or watch a plane or a bird flying in the air.
Wednesday	• Listen to upbeat music and dance to it. Have a good time. • Smell a few things during the day that have a strong smell, such as soap, shower gel, or some light perfume sprayed on clothes.
Thursday	• Help your child to lie on top of a bigger sized ball. Roll them and help them to keep their balance on the ball. Let them try to climb on and off. Be careful when doing this activity. Keep a good hold of your child while he or she is on the ball. • Build a wall using 6-9 blocks making sure your child sees what you are doing. Now place a few blocks in front of your child and encourage them to build a wall too.
Friday	• If you can play an instrument, play the melody of a short song, or else listen to a tune that is played on a flute or a recorder on a music CD. • Look at pictures of people in magazines. Name the clothes they are wearing.

Monday	• Do exercises, pull at something together and wrestle a bit. • Ask her to follow instructions: 'Give it to me, please', 'Bring it here', 'Put it in'. See if she has improved since the last time.
Tuesday	• Put a small box with a fold-up lid in front of her. Beforehand, put a toy in it. • Put a smaller towel on the floor. Put a toy on it and roll it up. Watch how she starts to look for it. Teach her how to roll up the towel herself.
Wednesday	• Put some rice cereal in a jar. Put the lid on loosely, and then show her how to take it off. • Listen to some music lying on the floor. If she gets up try to calm her down by stroking or scratching her gently.
Thursday	• Give her a spoon and let her practise eating. The food should be creamy so it stays on the spoon. • Cover the child with a shawl or scarf. Play peek-a-boo.
Friday	• Play ball. Roll it and hunt for it. • Watch vehicles outdoors.

Monday	• Put objects of various sizes into each other. • Talk on a toy phone.
Tuesday	• Take your child to a pet shop or the zoo where she can see fish and birds. • Let her nibble at rice cereal or small pieces of sweetbread.
Wednesday	• Build structures together using building blocks. • Place a small object on a tray and encourage her to carry it.
Thursday	• Look at a book with animal pictures. Tell her what the animals say. • Put some rice cakes/crackers in a narrow cup so it is difficult to get them out.
Friday	• Recite a rhyme banging to the beat. Ask her to clap as well. 'Humpty Dumpty Sat on a wall, Humpty Dumpty Had a great fall; All the king's horses And all the king's men, Couldn't put Humpty Together again.' • Sprinkle water out of a container that has a small hole in it.

4th week

Monday

- Sing a short song to her.
- Act out a scene using puppets or whistling animal toys. (The topic of your play: sleeping, washing.)

Tuesday

- Allow her to play with sieves, pots, spoons or lids. Ask for the objects one by one so you can see whether she knows their names. If not, you can name them for her.

- Give her a wet cloth so that she can wipe the floor with it. Mop the floor together.

Wednesday

- Build a garage. Push the cars inside.
- Look at a newspaper. Do not let her crumple it.

Thursday

- Put a heavy object in one of the child's hands and a light object in the other. Ask her: 'Light? Heavy?'
- Put a toy inside a see-through container. Allow her to play with it and teach her how to screw off the top and pour out the toy.

Friday

- Listen to a clock ticking: 'tic-tock'. Repeat the sound in front of her a few times. Stretch your arms and move to the beat.
- Practise naming the body parts. Look in the mirror: 'Where's your hair? Where are your eyes, ears?'

During the 13th month repeat the activities above

Description of the child
at the end of the 1st year

Height: cm/inch

Weight: kg/lbs

Foot size: cm/inch

Some of her features:

Some of her words (if she has any):

Typical activities:

Favourite toys:

Favourite food:

Favourite songs/nursery rhymes:

Developmental activities
for children aged 14-24 months

Children at the age of one are at very different levels of their development. Some of them are able to walk safely, while others are only trying to stand up. Their intellectual abilities are different as well, though there are certain tasks that most children of this age can carry out.

This list of activities, which is 10 months long and finishes when the child is 2, is meant to cater for a child with average developmental abilities.
Of course, you can do the tasks with a child who can only crawl, but you will need to omit the tasks that require the ability to stand or walk.

It isn't imperative that you do the tasks only for the actual age of your child.
You can go back to the activities listed for the previous months or move forward to the next bit. Take your pick from the next list if your child is able for it.
The time for the daily activities should not be less than half an hour. During this period do 2 or 3 tasks, out of which one should be either reading a story or playing with puppets. When reading the stories, talk freely and use puppets or teddies. This makes the story more interactive and interesting for the child, instead of a straightforward read aloud activity. Involve the child in the story telling by asking her to look at the pictures and by asking questions, for example: 'Where's the cat? Which is the cat's bowl?' It isn't necessary to do the activities within one session. You can do them on different occasions.

At the end of each play period spend a few minutes on carrying out the task of the month.

Motor skills
Speech
Intellectual skills
Emotional wellbeing
Independent play

I have planned 20 tasks for each month, according to the number of working days. On Saturdays and Sundays there should be free play and walks. Do not do sessions on these days.
If you miss a few days for whatever reason, just mark those tasks in the book and get back to them another time.

Areas of development

During this period of life there are no clearly divided phases in the child's development like there were during the first year. A certain daily routine has been established and her days – if she is healthy – go by in a usual order. Changes in the daily routine do not cause problems like they used to. Feeding the child has become easier too as now she can eat nearly everything that grown-ups eat.

Parents need to pay great attention to all her moves after the acquisition of independent walking. The development of a child aged 1-2 years can be divided into four sections: mastering of movements, establishment of speech, development of thinking and enrichment of emotional wellbeing.

We can help the least in the area of improving the movements, and teaching how to walk. The speed of this depends on the development of the child's bone structure, muscles and balancing skills.

Encourage your child's attempts to achieve independence. However, it is completely useless to try to make a child who can't even stand yet walk for a long time. It is impossible for the child to learn to walk on her own until she stands firmly on her feet. Let's have a look at a few exercises that could strengthen her legs and make her hands work better:

 Exercises for developing bodily awareness and motion skills
- Hold the child's hands and make her dance to the beat of a rhythmic rhyme, for example, 'Ring-a-ring o'roses, A pocket full of posies, A-tishoo! A-tishoo! We all fall down.'
- Encourage her to walk by showing her an interesting object.
- Roll balls with her.
- Make her pick up flat objects (a rice cake, a disc) to practise her fine motor skills.
- Build a castle using blocks. (Do this activity often, as the typical play of this period is practice play. Building and destroying is a good way for her to gain experience.)
- Try to put objects of various sizes into each other. (Three cups will do.)
- Roll a ball down a slope.
- Try to do shape recognition. Make a shape sorter by drawing around a mixture of building blocks (a cube, a cone and a prism) on a cardboard box and cutting the shapes out. Show your child which block belongs to which hole and push them through. First do it together, then she will be able to play on her own. (This activity is recommended from 18 months on.)
- Put a stick through hoops of various sizes.
- Give her a pencil or a piece of chalk, and teach her how to scribble.

- Offer her a chance to work with play dough or clay.
- She should have a toy car big enough for loading/unloading objects into/out of.
- She should get some building toy in which the pieces can be put together, but not Lego just yet.
- Let her eat independently with a spoon or a fork.
- Allow her to drink from a plastic cup alone.
- Teach her the notion of heavy and light. Ask her to lift the empty shopping basket, and then another one with things in it.
- Teach her how structures around the house open and close (for example, doors and wardrobe doors, drawers). You can prevent a lot of accidents this way.
- Teach her to obey when she hears: 'Stop!' Practise this a lot as accidents can be prevented if the child obeys this instruction unconditionally. Put her back into the buggy in the street until she learns to stop.
- In a sand box show her how to play with a sieve and a shovel and how to flatten the sand.
- Hunt for crumbs and pieces of paper on the floor.
- Place a block or another small object on top of her head to balance.
- Give her tasks that involve balancing, for example, carrying a plastic cup half full of water from one place to another.

 Speech development

It is important to talk to the child a lot, but what's most important is that she is listened to. The interested attention you give her when she speaks is much more persuasive than instructions. Never teach speech like this: 'Here's your hot chocolate. Say: Hot chocolate.' This kind of military style isn't appropriate for children.

Speech development should be embedded in play, too. First, practise short links of sounds:
- Listen to the clock ticking: tic-tock. Move your head to the beat. Try to make her play too.
- Knock on the door: 'Knock-knock. Who's knocking?'
- Keep on doing the imitation of animal sounds. Picture books as well as plastic animal figures are suitable for this activity.
- Use one- or two-word-long instructions, such as: 'Give me. Pick up. I want. Thank you. Bring here. Come here. Stop!'
- Rhymes and poems play a prominent part in speech development. Brush up on the ones she already knows. Your child will turn out to be a grateful audience.

- A few ideas: 'See-saw, Margery Daw'; 'Two little dicky birds'; 'Here we go round the Mulberry Bush'; 'The wheels on the bus'; 'Head, shoulders, knees and toes'; 'Fuzzy Wuzzy'; 'Horsie, Horsie' etc.
- Puppetry is very useful in the field of speech development and the improvement of thinking. One or two puppets are enough, and they can even be home made. An 18-24-month-old child can easily understand a short scene performed with puppets. The hand-held puppets encourage the child to try to make them talk herself.
- Listening to musical children's CDs and story CDs should be continued during this period.
- The child can watch TV or a video for a short while, about 10-15 minutes daily. You should pick a cartoon with no violence in it.
- Look at books with pictures of animals, people and objects daily. Besides naming objects, you can now talk about what's happening in the pictures.
- Do not use baby language. Teach your child words used by grown-ups. It is pointless to teach the child 'two languages'. The car should not be 'vroom-vroom', etc.

Improvement of intellectual skills

The improvement of the child's intellectual skills becomes possible by developing her thinking, her attention and her memory skills, as well as forming her creativity.

Attention is the primary condition of learning. Learning skills can be expanded both in quality and quantity by concentrating the child's attention and enhancing its permanence. That's why it is important to improve attention.

Memory skills help us recall things that are known to us from the past and coordinate these pieces of information. For small children the right method for improving memory skills is remembering and practising things. The repetition of games and tasks leaves a deeper imprint, which can be recollected more reliably later.

Creativity, or in other words the skill to make things up, is a necessity in our modern world. Help the child go beyond merely thinking along patterns and strive to come up with a variety of solutions. She should be encouraged to look for and try out alternatives.

Activities:
• Cover her favourite toy with a cloth in front of her. If she doesn't take the cloth off, you uncover it for her.
• Hide the toy behind you and let her see where it's gone. Ask her to find it.
• Place a small object on your open palm and then close your fist and watch if she looks for it. If she is not interested show her the toy again and hide it once more.
• Take two boxes and put something into one of them, while she's watching. Then cover the boxes.
• Play this game with three boxes.
• Change the place of the covered box. Encourage the child to look. If she manages to find the object even now give her praise, as this task needed a lot of attention.
• Tie a rope around a hoop or other toys and ask her to get them by pulling.
• Place an interesting looking toy outside of the cot or playpen and give her a stick or a hook that she can use to get it. If she cannot manage to get it, help her by showing her what to do.
• Place two boxes on the table and a few objects of different qualities, for example, blocks and balls. Show her how to sort them. She might try it after a while.

- Practise sorting using objects in two different colours, for example, red and yellow buttons or discs.
- Create a pattern in front of her by putting objects (buttons) next to each other.

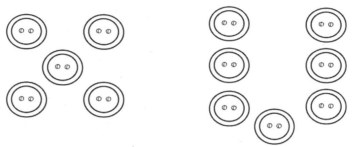

- Count objects up to three (cubes, cylinders, etc.).
- Continue to teach her the body parts: 'Where's your head?', 'Where's your neck?', 'Where's your tummy?' If she needs help place her hand on the appropriate part of the body. Continue practising using pictures of people. Body parts for teaching during the early days are: head, neck, tummy, chest, arm and leg. Later you can practise finer details like: nose, eye, mouth, tooth, tongue, hair, elbow, wrist, fingers, nail, knee, ankle, foot and belly button.
- Teach your child the names of pieces of furniture. A child at the age of 18-24 months can understand simple instructions. Use her willingness to help and give her simple tasks, for example, 'Put it in the fridge', 'Take it to the bath tub', 'Put it in the drawer'.
- Let her help with the housework. It's a great way to gain useful experiences, and she will enjoy helping you and being praised for her assistance. She can help by watering plants, dusting, doing the laundry, doing the dishes, mopping, kneading dough (all under your careful supervision).
- Acquaint her with natural substances, such as soil, sand and gravel.
- Play together with sand. Teach her how to build a pile, how to smooth it, how to make a hole in it, how to draw on it and how to press something on it. Teach her to shovel, sieve, rake and 'make a cake'.
- Take her to the garden or the market. Give her fruits and vegetables and name them. You can test her knowledge by looking at picture books as well, for example: 'Which one is the apple?', 'Which is the carrot?'

- When out walking show her flowers, leaves, grass, trees, shrubs.
- Show her ants, snails, bugs, butterflies, frogs, grasshoppers, crickets, sparrows, swallows, herons, pigeons.
- Take her to a water bank where she can watch the movement of the water. Let her throw something in it (ensure she is a safe distance away from the water at all times).
- When at the beach or in a pool, give her a cup or a bucket that she can use to scoop the water with.
- Name vehicles to her: cars, trucks, trams, buses, bicycles, motorbikes, ships, planes, helicopters, etc.
- Acquaint her with the area around your home. Walk the same route often. Name what's there to see.
- Focus her attention on small things. Look at fish in a tank. Watch how cats and dogs behave. Watch insects or an ants' nest for a few minutes.
- The most suitable accessories for improving creativity are the ones that are variable themselves, for instance, construction kits.
- Teach your child how to build things consciously. Encourage her to talk about what she's going to build and put down the simple structures according to the plan. You too should take part in the process at the beginning.
- Playing with play dough holds huge potential. At the start, you should form simple shapes, for example, worms, snails, small bowls. Use buttons, matchsticks, cloves, peppercorns, dry flowers, etc. to decorate your pieces.
- Show her how to make a montage – cut pictures out of newspapers, magazines or old books. Let the child arrange these pictures, then make a new picture out of them and stick the pieces on. Talk about these montages and make up stories.
- Start giving your child 'drawing classes'. Start with simple shapes.
- Give her a pencil, crayons or a piece of chalk when outdoors so that she can experiment with drawing. Draw some simple lines yourself, and then ask your child to try it too. If you want, you can make a nice, colourful joint picture.
- Show your child shadow theatre. Use the shadows from sunlight or a lamp and cast shadows/shapes on the wall.
- The more information the child gets about her surroundings, the more confident, constructive and imaginative she will become later. This thirst for knowledge, learning and the joy gained from play and her explorations will mean a great motivational force in later years also.

Enriching emotional wellbeing

A child around 1 year of age is able to express a number of emotions through her non-verbal channels. Her life of independence starts when she learns how to walk. Her parents do not pick her up as often as they used to, so the physical contact between parent and child gets reduced. Often kisses become scarcer than during her first year of life. Conflicts deriving from the child's new behaviour patterns (for instance, rearranging things, liveliness) can lead to emotional changes. The child needs to feel their parental love every moment, even in conflict situations.

Here are a few words on aggression. You may ask: 'Is it something we need to talk about when thinking about a one-year-old?' The answer is yes, because this is the period when some children might receive their first slaps on their hands, bum or face. This kind of physical discipline must be avoided at all costs. Not only is it upsetting for a child, but it is also confusing. The child is usually a victim of temper. Children benefit from discipline that is verbal. They benefit and understand when they are told 'No' or 'Stop' and told why. They also benefit and are more likely to understand when they are removed from a situation or have a toy removed. Aggression towards the child is an abuse of her weakness and vulnerability. There is a complex danger in the case of children who experience aggression and beating from their guardians. It can cause the child to become estranged from her parents, which may result in behaviour problems at a later stage. On the other hand, parental example to the child works like a guideline for social orientation. A child who is physically punished for her mistakes cannot find an alternative when trying to deal with conflicts with her mates.

Using words is clearer for a child. Explain things to your child patiently and forbid things if necessary (take her toy away, put her in her room etc.) but do not hit her.

Advice on enriching the emotional life and creating balance:
• Take her to the mirror after putting on nice, clean clothes. Tell her and show her how good she looks. This will reinforce a positive self-image.
• Whenever you can have a play fight in bed. Caress and hug her, and pretend to 'chew' her. This can be a good relaxation technique for both of you.
• Start to make bedtime stories regular. The child's nervous system benefits from the motherly or fatherly caressing while listening to a short calming song or gentle humming. If the child falls asleep and sleeps peacefully it will make her more balanced.

- At this stage of her life a child has a well-developed ability to detect mood. Take this into consideration when trying to shape her emotional life. Strive for creating a relaxed, happy and loving atmosphere in the family.
- Prevent her from seeing over-stimulating, violent or loud scenes on TV.
- Conflicts in the family should not be settled while she is around.
- Teach her how to express love towards others. Do not laugh when she hugs or kisses her friends or cousins, but encourage it.
- Pick her up whenever she asks you to, as this means that she needs reassurance.
- Expressing love should have a place in your play activities as well, for example, the toy animals can kiss and hug each other when they meet.
- Show her examples of expressing joy.
- If she gives you something thank her for it. You can also stroke her, give her a kiss or give her a bright smile.
- Put nice clothes on her for special occasions.
- Everything should suggest that her birthday or Christmas time is different from an ordinary day. It doesn't matter if she doesn't understand what's happening. She will be mesmerised by the magic in the air. Do not deprive yourselves of these positive moments.
- Teach her to appreciate and value new or nice things.
- Do not let her play in inappropriate clothes; put on old clothes when out playing in the sand, etc.
- She should value a nice card or a book.
- Do not allow her to scribble in books or to crush them. If she attempts to do this take the book away and explain why.
- After tidying up the child's room draw her attention to it. This will help her notice nice, clean and tidy things.
- Story telling using pictures should become part of the daily activities more and more often. When telling a story make sure you use a variety of tones of voice, volume and facial expressions. These elements promote the understanding of the story as well as the successful transmission of the mood. Choose stories that reflect joy and happiness. Later, you can also acquaint your child with notions of sadness, compassion and sorrow through this type of story telling.

Forming independent play

It is advisable to keep the time for independent play as part of the routine for a walking child. If she has grown out of her playpen, you can put up a safety gate at the door of the child's room or another room in the house, so that she can retire here while playing on her own. She still needs these play periods; they are also important for her development. If you have a big living room or a good sized kitchen you can fence off a corner for independent play.

A child aged between 1-2 years, who has been encouraged to play independently, can become immersed in an activity quite well. The parent might have a difficult job thinking of new ideas and ways to encourage the child to initiate playing on her own. The child can reach every toy in every corner of the room, so there is no point organising activity boxes for her any more. There are still simple ways of holding her interest with the toys you already have - examine the stock of toys every month and take most of the objects off the shelves. There shouldn't be more than 10-15 types of toys in the room. The rest should be put in a box and then, after a few weeks, they can be welcomed as new toys by the child.

What kind of toys hold the child's interest the most? This hugely depends on the personality and habits of the child. You should always leave a construction kit, small animal toys, 1-2 dolls, a bigger car, a dumper truck to load, a pull along animal, toys to screw or spin around, a bucket, a stacking assortment and books with rigid pages in the room. You can add a few pieces from the kitchen to the toy collection every day: plastic containers, boxes, spoons, pots and lids, etc. She can have some music on in the background. Relaxing music, children's songs or a nursery rhyme CD often work well.

Make the time for independent play last half an hour to an hour. Of course, if the child doesn't enjoy it do not force it on her. Try starting an activity together and when she seems to have got used to it leave her. Encourage her to stay in one room or outside when she is having her independent play. Ensure that it is safe and that she is not wandering around the house unsupervised.

Now is also a good time to encourage her to tidy up her toys by showing her and asking her to help you. Under no circumstances should you let the child come and go around the house all day leaving a big mess behind. Children who do not learn how to play will later have difficulties in accepting social regulations. If possible, take the child outside to play, but even in this case there should be an objective to her activities rather than just running around destroying things.

Independent play is part of the child's psychological development. And though the child is trying to carry out an increasing amount of tasks on her own (eating, dressing), in her play, interestingly, she seems to need company. Indeed, togetherness during a free style activity gives her reassurance and a sense of contentment. She needs to be persuaded (by trials and training) to play independently. By showing her how to pull the laces through the holes of a shoe or how to empty things out of a box we can give the child, who seems to be attached to parental company, the tools for independent play. Do not give in every time she wants something; firmly but calmly make her let you have some free time. This must be understood by every member of the family in order to avoid the child getting somebody else to play with her. A child's strong personality can be counterbalanced by a firm and consistent parenting style. Parents should not always give in. There needs to be boundaries for a child to develop in a healthy way. These boundaries need to be consistent and clear, so she understands what she can and cannot do. If we give in one time and don't give in the next time this will cause confusion and will make the child feel uncertain. If she knows that there is some flexibility, she will start fights or initiate arguments that she will eventually win. Of course, if she spends her playtime crying, then the independent play needs to be examined and maybe started over again using smaller amounts of time.

Arising problems must be handled with love and appropriate firmness. We must be prepared for this and instead of choosing the easier way of instinctive reactions or giving in, we should stick to the more difficult, conscious decisions, as this will benefit both parent and child in the long run.

Sets of activities for children aged 14-24 months

Activity set 1 for 14 (13-15) months of age

TASK OF THE MONTH
To recognise ten toys by their name. Choose three objects then ask:
'Give me the doll.' Keep these toys together so it's easy to get them when you do
the activity over the month.

1st week

Monday	• Hold the child's hand and march to the beat of a rhyme or song, for example: 'Here we go round the Mulberry Bush'; 'Humpty Dumpty'.
Tuesday	• Roll a ball.
Wednesday	• Play on her fingers: 'This little piggy'.
Thursday	• Talk on a toy phone. 'Hello, hello, how are you?'
Friday	• Play with rice cakes/crackers or oat cakes. Put one in a cup on the table. Cover the cracker with a cup.

2nd week

Monday	• Let her play in the bath with a cup: scoop water out and pour it into another dish.
Tuesday	• Communicate using head movements (yes – no).
Wednesday	• Stick your tongue out. Copy each other.
Thursday	• Listen to the clock ticking and say: tic-tock. Move to the beat.
Friday	• Build a simple castle for the child. Let *her* put the blocks on each other, too.

3rd week

Monday	• Practise the body parts. 'Where's your head, hand, leg, tummy, eye, nose, mouth, ear?'
Tuesday	• Sing songs: 'Hickory, dickory, dock'; 'Incy Wincy'.
Wednesday	• Play with objects by putting them into each other.
Thursday	• Teach her the names of some kitchen equipment. Place a plastic spoon, a cup, a plate, a sieve, etc. on the floor. Ask the child: 'Hand me the cup.' etc.
Friday	• Crawl and pick up crumbs and pieces of paper off the floor. (If needed you can tear a small sheet of paper into pieces and throw them down beforehand).

4th week

Monday	• Play hide and seek with puppets. When it appears say: 'here, there'. Wave bye-bye at the window.
Tuesday	• Let her eat small pieces of bread or cereal, etc. by hand.
Wednesday	• Watch snails and insects outside. Show her soil, gravel and a stick. (Let her hold these).
Thursday	• Make faces at and copy each other.
Friday	• Listen to good music and dance to it together.

TASK OF THE MONTH
To practise drinking from a cup.

1st week

Monday	• Teach her how to screw the top on and off a plastic container.
Tuesday	• Cough and say: 'bad cough'. Sneeze and say: 'a-tchoo'. Ask the child to copy you.
Wednesday	• Practise the names of various rooms in the house. 'Go to the living room!'; 'I'm here, come to the kitchen'; 'Take this to the bathroom!' etc.
Thursday	• Look at pictures of animals in a book and imitate the sounds they make. Choose domestic animals.
Friday	• Sing children's songs. Move to the rhythm.

2nd week

Monday	• Play with play dough. (You can use homemade dough, too.) Show her how to make a ball and how to flatten it.
Tuesday	• Hide an object behind you in a way that the child can see what's happening. Ask her to look for it.
Wednesday	• Build a garage for small cars.
Thursday	• Act out a short scene with puppets. (Plastic animals will do as well.) The topic can be: movements – standing, lying and running).
Friday	• Look in the mirror and name details of your face. The child should point to the eye, nose, etc. on your face, for example: 'Where's mummy's eye?' Look into a full size mirror, move around and name your body parts.

3rd week

Monday	• First, you sort the building blocks yourself, and later involve the child, too. Make two groups: cylinders and bricks.
Tuesday	• Put hoops of various sizes on a stick. (You can also buy a set like this.) Do not worry about the sizes just yet.
Wednesday	• Roll a ball. Lay the child on top of a bigger ball and roll her.
Thursday	• Place a pillow on the head of the sitting child so that she can balance it while moving.
Friday	• Make her lift heavy and light objects. Say: 'Heavy, light'. Push a toy car slowly, and then give it a big fast push. Say: 'Slow, fast'.

Fable

4th week

Monday	• Listen to a CD and dance together.
Tuesday	• Ask her to help with the housework. She can dry the dishes or wipe the floor or table with a wet cloth.
Wednesday	• Give her a pencil or some crayons and let her scribble.
Thursday	• Knock at the door: knock-knock. Clap hands: clap-clap.
Friday	• If the weather is nice build a sand castle. Shovel the sand in one heap, smooth the sides, and stick a leaf or a flower on the top.

TASK OF THE MONTH
To practise eating with a spoon.

1st week

Monday	• Do exercises. Teach her how to draw circles with her arms, and how to bend and straighten them. Squat and stand up. Move around on your hands and knees.
Tuesday	• Say nursery rhymes, for example, 'Baa-baa, black sheep'. (Look for lovely rhymes in books to say together.)
Wednesday	• Sort beans or other objects: separate the whites from the dark ones by putting them into different bowls.
Thursday	• Go to another house and visit family or friends. Allow her to make friends with people not in her immediate family.
Friday	• Play with cars. Make engine sounds. Act out a short scene using the car and a few passenger toys.

2nd week

Monday	• Cut some nice and colourful pictures out of magazines. Let her arrange them as she likes but do not allow her to crush them. Stick the best arrangements on sheets and display them on the wall.
Tuesday	• While out walking watch small creatures: spiders, ladybirds or ants.
Wednesday	• Repeat the 'warm-cold' game in the bath. Put floating and sinking objects in her water and ask her to collect them.
Thursday	• Listen to music; bang to the beat. (If she's not able yet, hold her hands and help.)
Friday	• Play with the light switch when it's dark. Say: 'dark, bright'.

3rd week

Monday	• Play with play dough. Teach her how to roll a ball. Show her how to make a worm and a circle. 
Tuesday	• Let her help you with the housework: to do the laundry or to tidy up.
Wednesday	• Throw down buttons or big pieces of paper and ask her to collect them in her dumper truck.
Thursday	• Give her a pencil or crayons so she can scribble.
Friday	• Ask her to follow instructions, for example, 'Put it on the table'; 'Bring the basket here'; 'Take the apple to daddy'.

4th week

Monday	• Put pickled gherkins in front of her and ask her to have a taste. After that let her taste a sugar cube. Tell her the different tastes: 'sweet' and 'sour'.
Tuesday	• Pick up leaves and sticks while out walking. Show her how to use the stick to draw on the ground.
Wednesday	• Practise the instructions: 'Stop!' and 'Come here!' in a safe place.
Thursday	• Use building blocks to build a structure as high as possible.
Friday	• Place two cups in front of her and put a rice cake into one of them. Make sure she sees it. Cover the cups. See if she finds the rice cake straight away. Practise this three or four times. 

Activity set 4 for 17 (16-18) months of age

TASK OF THE MONTH
To practise naming body parts using toy animals.

1st week

Monday	• Put the child on your lap, hold her hands and let her lean back so she sees the world upside down.
Tuesday	• Sort buttons according to colour. (Use only two colours.)
Wednesday	• Copy each other: stroke her hair and ask her to do the same. Make a smiley face and get serious.
Thursday	• Ask her to smell different scents: Say: nice smell, stinky, etc.
Friday	• Let her clean her room, do some dusting and wipe the bars of her cot with a wet cloth. If possible, visit children of the same age.

2nd week

Monday	• Build a train out of building blocks. Push it along carefully so it doesn't fall apart.
Tuesday	• Tell a story using a picture book. Ask the child about what's happening in the pictures. Learn action words: which animal is running, lying, swimming?
Wednesday	• Throw some rice or lentils on the table in front of the child and ask her to collect them in a small bowl.
Thursday	• Do exercises. Lie on your back, lift your legs and arms and wiggle them a few times.
Friday	• Go down on all fours and imitate animals. Touch heads and push, crawl after one another and chase: 'We are dogs' – bark, crow and grunt.

3rd week

Monday	• Look in the mirror and make faces.
Tuesday	• Teach her how to turn the pages in a regular book. Look at the pages and name what you see using only one word at a time.
Wednesday	• Play with play dough. Make balls, and put them on top of each other. Decorate the snowman with peppercorns and cloves. Use a top for a medicine bottle as a hat, if you have it. 
Thursday	• Dramatise a few nursery rhymes. Pick a tickly one, too. ('Round and round the garden')
Friday	• Listen to music and dance.

4th week

Monday	• Show her how to open and close doors, wardrobe doors and drawers safely.
Tuesday	• Practise how to put things into each other. 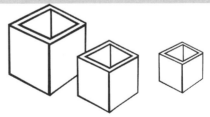
Wednesday	• Draw straight lines with a pencil. Draw a fence together.
Thursday	• Practise instructions: 'Stop!' and 'Come here!'
Friday	• Smack your lips, and say simple words (word pairs) that describe sounds: knock-knock, tic-tock, splish-splash, ring-ring and bang-bang.

Activity set 5 for 18 (17-19) months of age

TASK OF THE MONTH
To get familiar with pieces of furniture in the room.
First: 'We're pulling the curtains' and 'Let's put it on the bed'.
Later: 'Pull the curtains' and 'Put it on the bed', etc.

1st week

Monday	• Give her black paper and chalk, or plain paper and coloured pencils, so that she can scribble.
Tuesday	• Take a walk near some water: watch how it moves and throw stones in it. Smell some flowers.
Wednesday	• Hide objects so that the child can look for them. Put some toys under a shawl, behind your back, on top of a cupboard, or in a drawer. Practise opening and closing doors and drawers.
Thursday	• Play: 'This little piggy'. Count the fingers (up to five).
Friday	• Check if she knows the names of her body parts: 'Where's your head, hand, tummy, leg, neck, ear, hair, nose and eye?'

2nd week

Monday	• Build a house using blocks, and play with it with dolls, cars and animals.
Tuesday	• Look at animal pictures in a book that the child is already familiar with. Check if she knows their names by asking questions. Imitate animal sounds.
Wednesday	• Place some toys or food further away from the child so that she cannot reach them. Give her a tool to get them, for example, a stick, a ruler or a spoon. If she doesn't make an attempt, show her how to achieve her goal.
Thursday	• Turn the light on and off saying: 'bright, dark'. Show her a shadow on the wall and get her to focus her attention on it.
Friday	• Roll a ball down a slope. Bounce the ball in front of you and then throw it to each other from a short distance.

3rd week

Monday
- Play with play dough. Make a snake family. Show her how she can poke the flat dough with a pencil or a matchstick.

Tuesday
- Look at a magazine together. Talk about what you see.

Wednesday
- Pick three cylinders, three pyramids and three bricks out of the building block set.
  Build three identical structures.

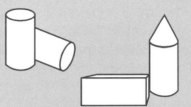

Thursday
- Trace the outline of a cylinder (the circular base of the cylinder) and a cube on a cardboard sheet. Cut it out and place the cardboard on top of a box. Show the child how to push the blocks through the holes. This is the beginning of the shape sorting exercise.

Friday
- Concentrate her attention on small things: watch fish in a tank, snails or an ant colony.

4th week

Monday
- Do exercises to music. Practise very simple movements, such as: circling with your arms, bends, walking and crawling around in a circle.

Tuesday
- Place three cups in front of her and put a rice cake into one of them before covering them. See if she can find it straight away. Practise this three or four times.

Wednesday
- Sing short songs.
  Clap her small hands to the beat.

Thursday
- Let her practise scooping the water in the bath and picking objects up from the bottom of the tub.

Friday
- Involve her in doing the housework. Allow her to do dusting, or wipe the floor with a wet cloth, etc.

TASK OF THE MONTH
To practise walking up and down the stairs.

1st week

Monday	• Let her start getting familiar with the colours. Sort red and yellow buttons or toys apart. Name the colours often, and then check her knowledge by asking questions.
Tuesday	• Put toys in a number of places in the room when the child is not looking. Ask her to follow instructions, such as, 'Bring Teddy here from the table' or 'Take your rabbit from the armchair', etc.
Wednesday	• Show her small insects while out walking; pull out a bunch of grass and watch birds.
Thursday	• Get to know the body parts. 'Here's your elbow, your ankle, your eyebrow.' Then later: 'Where's your elbow?' 'Where's your ankle?' etc.
Friday	• Visit friends. Feel free to use the word 'No!' outside of your home.

2nd week

Monday	• Cut 3 or 4 pictures of smaller animals and cars out of magazines. Stick them on a blank sheet together. Let the child help with arranging the pictures.
Tuesday	• Put buttons next to each other in a row together: you put one down, and then the child puts one down.
Wednesday	• Teach her how to step (perhaps jump) over a pillow, a piece of string or a toy.
Thursday	• Watch vehicles during your walk. Name and show her cars, trucks, bicycles, motorbikes, trams and buses.
Friday	• Listen to music and dance with toy animals.

3rd week

Monday	• Practise the sorting exercises that you started last month. (Use only two different shapes!)
Tuesday	• Play with play dough. You can make balls and roll out cylinders and let her stick cloves and bay leaves all over them.
Wednesday	• Get familiar with vegetables in the garden or at the market. Offer her some raw tomatoes, peppers, carrots and cucumbers to eat.
Thursday	• Rest together and play with the shadows of your hands on the wall. Hold the child's hand and move it so she recognises the shadow of her own hand.
Friday	• Look at a picture book and talk about what's in it. Say short sentences naming the actions as well as the subject, for example, 'The bird's flying'.

4th week

Monday	• Play with toys: put three toy animals around the 'table' and place a plate, a napkin, a piece of cake and a spoon in front of each of the animals. Count everything separately.
Tuesday	• Do some drawing. You can draw clouds, a sun and flowers. Let the child scribble, too. Use a bigger sheet so that both of you can 'work' on the same sheet.
Wednesday	• Do exercises to music. Show her how to squat down, jump in one place, turn her head around and wave her legs.
Thursday	• Place three cups in front of her. Put a cracker or a rice cake into one of them. Cover all three cups and mix them up. See if she finds the cup with the treat in it. Practise this three or four times.
Friday	• Go walking and collect stones, chestnuts or acorns. Arrange them in a long row or a heap. Walk between the objects along the row without stepping on them.

TASK OF THE MONTH
To build a different structure every day using building blocks.

1st week

Monday	• Tie a piece of string around a toy and show her how to pull it to get the toy. Let her pull it behind her even in the street.
Tuesday	• Practise shape sorting. You should still use only two shapes at a time, but pick new ones, different from the previous two. Trace around, for example, circular and triangular objects.
Wednesday	• Build a castle together; encourage her to use all of the building blocks.
Thursday	• Look at and name pictures of vehicles in a book. Encourage her to make the sound of the vehicle, for example, 'beep, beep', 'choo, choo', 'vroom, vroom'. Try to assess how well she knows them.
Friday	• Look at a pack of cards. Play with distributing them: one for you, one for her. Put down two cards at a time, and then put cards down in various ways, for example, one after another, one next to another or on top of each other like stairs.

2nd week

Monday	• Play imitation. Make a serious face followed by a happy one. Stick your tongue out and goggle your eyes. Wait until the child starts to copy you and then you start copying her.
Tuesday	• Involve her in doing the housework by giving instructions: 'Please bring it here!', 'Take it there!' and 'Put it on the table!'
Wednesday	• Listen to music together; bang to the beat on the bed or on the table. Have a laugh and wrestle a bit with each other in a light playful manner.
Thursday	• Play with play dough. Allow her to mix two colours.
Friday	• Practise the colours. She already knows yellow and red, now you can show her blue. Cut coloured cards up into pieces and sort these according to colour. Make a tri-colour montage by sticking the pieces on a sheet.

3rd week

Monday	• During your walk observe small animals, various leaves, and smell some flowers. Take her to a place where she can pick flowers. Teach her how to pick them one by one, and how to hold them by the stems.
Tuesday	• Look at picture books with pictures of objects in them. Check how well she knows them.
Wednesday	• Play with toy animals. Build a home for them, take them for a drive, take them to the doctor and feed them. Bring them to life with words.
Thursday	• Buy a bag of colourful beads. Give her small bowls so that she can arrange the beads in them. (Ensure she doesn't put them in her mouth.)
Friday	• Learn about fruit and vegetables. Let her eat raw carrot, apple, and other fruit and vegetables. Talk about red and yellow fruit and vegetables. 

4th week

Monday	• Visit people where she is encouraged to communicate with others.
Tuesday	• Roll a ball. Try to throw it into a bucket from a short distance.
Wednesday	• Place three cups and three spoons in front of the child. Let her play with them. Put spoons in the cups, a different number each time, and count them.
Thursday	• Look for shoes of various sizes, for example, small shoes she's grown out of and big adult sizes. Ask her to try them on and walk in them. Compare them and practise the words 'small' and 'big'. 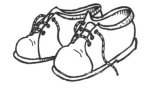
Friday	• Draw a stick man. Ask her to try it too.

TASK OF THE MONTH
To turn the pages of a newspaper or a book with non-rigid pages.

1st week

Monday	• Get a selection of objects with screw tops, for example, a face cream tub, a tube of toothpaste and a jar and put them in front of the child. Ask her to open them, and then ask her to close them.
Tuesday	• Look at pictures of women and men in a magazine, and name the pieces of clothing they are wearing. Practise recognising and naming clothes and shoes.
Wednesday	• Listen to some music and dance to it. You hum along and encourage her to hum along as well.
Thursday	• Play with toy animals and dolls, like you did in the previous month. Change their clothes and put them on the potty, if it's possible.
Friday	• Practise saying the body parts. Learn about where you find the knee, the wrist and the belly button.

2nd week

Monday	• Use brick-shaped blocks and cubes from the building block set, and build a long train. Sit a few toys on top of it and try to push it along. Encourage her to make the sound of a train.
Tuesday	• Put new objects in her bath, such as small cups, a funnel, a few buttons. Let her pick them out and play with them.
Wednesday	• Continue the shape sorting exercise. If sorting into two groups is going well, make the outline of three easily distinguishable but simple shapes.
Thursday	• Roll balls and slide cubes down slopes of various angles.
Friday	• Cut up a red, a yellow and a blue sheet and make a picture of a beautiful colourful bird out of the pieces, for example, a peacock or a parrot. Stick it on a blank sheet, and display it on the wall or on a tile.

3rd week

Monday	• Listen to a variety of sounds outdoors. 'Can you hear the trees rustling? Can you hear the blackbird singing? Can you hear the tram rumbling?', 'What else can you hear?'
Tuesday	• Place toys in a few rooms of the house in a central place, so that they can be spotted easily. Ask the child to collect them, for example, 'Go to the bathroom and pick up your teddy bear!'
Wednesday	• Place small pieces of food on a plate in front of the child (a cube of cheese, a piece of apple, a slice of salami, a pepper stick and a piece of rice cake). Give her another plate and ask her to put the ones that she wants to eat on it. It requires serious discipline not to take and eat them straight away.
Thursday	• Make a flower shape out of buttons. Stack the buttons until the 'tower' falls down.
Friday	• If possible, use a projector to read a story for her. Otherwise, read a short story from a picture book or use an audio tape book or a CD book.

4th week

Monday	• Build structures from the pieces of the building block set. Use these objects for situational games, for example, shopping, arranging the interior of the home, etc.)
Tuesday	• Play with play dough. Flatten it and fold up the edges, so that you have a bowl. Decorate it by pushing a stick into it or scraping it, and put colourful dough eggs in it.
Wednesday	• Do exercises. Teach her how to open her legs when she is standing, how to lean forward and how to wave her arms up and down.
Thursday	• Place objects in front of her out of reach and let her use a tool to pull them closer.
Friday	• Copy each other's movements, for example, scratch your head, blink, nod and shake your head.

TASK OF THE MONTH
To sing a song at the end of the playtime.

1st week

Monday	• Put out three boxes or cups – all of them should have a lid. Put a small object into one of them, and change its position, after covering the cups/boxes. It takes persistent attention from the child to find it.
Tuesday	• Practise the body parts using pictures. 'Where's the lady's neck, ear, elbow, ankle, eye?', etc.
Wednesday	• Build a castle that has three or four sides so it has a courtyard to play in. Place toy animals into the yard.
Thursday	• Read short poems from books.
Friday	• Do exercises: roll your head, stand on tiptoes, squat down and exercise your arms. Lie down on your side and roll back and forth.

2nd week

Monday	• Do the shape recognition exercise using two or three objects.
Tuesday	• Play with your hands and fingers: always a different finger should peek out of your closed fist.
Wednesday	• Put hoops of various sizes on a stick. Try to pick out the biggest one and put the rest of them on according to their size.
Thursday	• Do balancing exercises. Place a small pillow or a book on her head and ask her to walk with it. Give her a plastic cup full of water (not entirely full) and ask her to take it to a different room.
Friday	• Make an 'ikebana' (flower arrangement) using dried flowers. Allow her to stick the flower into a piece of play dough that she had shaped herself. Encourage her attempts.

3rd week

Monday
- Build a bed and a chair out of building blocks for toy animals or dolls. Play with them.

Tuesday
- Play imitation then hide and seek. Ask her to find you by listening to your voice. Cover her and you should try to find her as well.

Wednesday
- Work with crayons.
  Show her how to colour in a simple shape.

Thursday
- Play imitating animals. Go down on all fours and make animal sounds (dogs, cats, pigs, cows, goats, hens and cockerels).

Friday
- Sort some counters or buttons.
  Pay attention to their colour or their size.

4th week

Monday
- Play with dolls and animals.
  Take them to the doctor and drive them around in toy cars.

Tuesday
- Weather permitting, play in the sand box: teach her how to make a ball using wet sand. Build a sand castle.

Wednesday
- Play hiding a toy. Put the toy in various parts of the room and tell her where to look, for example, 'It's behind the armchair.'

Thursday
- Act out rhymes, 'Hickory dickory' ; 'Incy Wincy Spider'

Friday
- Go outside and watch small creatures moving around.

TASK OF THE MONTH
To practise following instructions.
Give her two or three tasks at the end of the playtime, for example,
'Put the toy back on the shelf' or 'Bring your shoes here'.

1st week

Monday	• Imitate each other's movements and facial expressions: open and close your mouth like fish do, roll your eyes around, nod, laugh and make a serious face.
Tuesday	• Give the child a selection of objects – they should be either hard or soft. Squash them and name the ones that are soft, and then name the hard ones. Ask the child to hand you the soft ones.
Wednesday	• Do shape recognition with three new objects. Pick ones which are circular, triangular or square shaped.
Thursday	• Read poems or rhymes from books.
Friday	• Clean and tidy up together. Give her a wet cloth, a brush, etc.

2nd week

Monday	• Talk on a toy phone.
Tuesday	• Arrange some cut out shapes and stick them on to make a picture. Let her arrange the pieces. A big butterfly image would look great on the wall!
Wednesday	• Play with a ball. Roll it and chase it.
Thursday	• Place small pieces of food in front of her on a plate. Ask her not to eat them yet. First, ask her to put aside the ones that she would like to eat. Later, name what they taste like, for example, 'sweet', 'sour', etc.
Friday	• Play with play dough. Teach her how to flatten the dough and make it even thinner by rolling it with a pencil and then show her how to roll the dough up on the pencil. Allow her to slice the dough with a blunt knife.

3rd week

Monday	• Sort buttons according to different qualities: look at their size and their colour. Make a row of patterns: white-red-white or small-big-small.
Tuesday	• Build a house that has four sides out of building blocks. (It should not be taller than 4 or 5 lines.) Make windows and a door and make the toys peep out.
Wednesday	• Do some exercises: skip and jump and teach your child how to do a forward tumble.
Thursday	• Colour a few pictures in from a colouring book.
Friday	• Play with a doll. Dress it in winter or summer clothes. Take it for a walk then put it into bed. 

4th week

Monday	• Listen to a few nursery songs. Dance or do some steps in one direction while facing each other and holding both hands.
Tuesday	• Put small and big objects in front of her, and ask her to give you a small object, then ask her for a big one. (Balls of play dough will do.)
Wednesday	• Sort picture play cards. Take out the identical pairs. Arrange the cards into various lines. You could build a card castle, then blow it away together.
Thursday	• Put floating toys into her bath and let her play with them. Use plastic containers for making bubbles and for sprinkling.
Friday	• 'Hunt' for pieces of paper and breadcrumbs. Collect them into a bucket or a toy truck.

Description of the child
at the end of the 2nd year

Height: cm/inch

Weight: kg/lbs

Foot size: cm/inch

Movements:

Some of her features:

Typical activities:

Favourite songs/nursery rhymes:

Some of the funny things she has said or done:

Speech development:

Favourite toys:

Favourite books:

Favourite food:

Developmental activities for children aged 24-36 months

After the child's second birthday, it is worth thinking about what knowledge and what forms of behaviour she will need to be able to integrate smoothly into the new social environment that playschool provides.

Motor skills
Speech
Intellectual skills
Emotional wellbeing
Independent play

Starting playschool is a big thing in every child's life. Even if the child had been attending a crèche and she is familiar with social routines, it is still a new challenge. Parents can do a lot during this year to assist and help their children in settling and enjoying the start of playschool. An easy transition into playschool will also help them to settle into school later on.

The year before they start playschool, whether at home, in a crèche, or childminder's, you can help them to be prepared. It is worth doing special activities in the crèche with children of this age group, as the reinforcing effect of that kind of work is a favourable thing.

Next, we are going to examine the possibilities of development support – just as we did for the previous year. The main areas of development are movements, thinking and emotional wellbeing.

After the thematic summaries you will find ten developmental day-to-day programmes for each month. Every day you should spend some time doing the task of the month.

Have fun and enjoy your work!

Possibilities in movement development

Most two-year-old children are able to walk and run safely. Sometimes stopping can cause a problem after a fast running period. Warn your child of this and show them how to slow down and stop without falling.

Movements can be divided into two major groups: gross motor movements and fine motor movements.

To support the development of gross motor skills the best thing is to let the child run and move around freely. However, running around improves stamina only. Here are some ways to improve your child's motor skills all round:

- Ball play offers an outstanding opportunity. To catch the ball requires great skill. Play rolling, throwing, target throwing, passing it to each other and kicking it into the goal.
- Both boys and girls should be taught how to play football.
- If possible, build an obstacle course out of 3 or 4 car tyres, which can be used for walking on, balancing or climbing through.
- Take the child to the beach or a swimming pool and start teaching her how to swim.
- Allow and encourage her to climb trees. (Explain the dangers of unsupervised play. Give the child a strict warning that dangerous exercises can only be done while you are around.)
- Do exercises to improve her movements once or twice a week. Do the following exercises: marching to music/some beat; standing on tiptoes, walking on tiptoes, walking club-footed (turn your feet inside and then turn them outside); jumping up from squatting; walking while squatting; walking on hands and knees; standing on one foot; arm exercises (rotating, bends); bending your body (forward, backward, to the sides); balancing at the edge of the rug or the footpath; lifting the arms and legs while lying on the back; lifting the arms and legs while lying on the tummy; letting the head down and lifting it up while on all fours, lifting the legs while on all fours.
- Dance to some beat.
- Let her ride a bicycle.
- Teach her how to push herself on the swings.
- Help her patiently get dressed and fold clothes.

Fine motor skill development:

Manipulative activities have a great importance even in the first year of the pre-school curriculum. Children who have gone through a good training programme can achieve a lot with these kinds of activities. Fine motor hand movements are not innate but can be acquired. Children who use their hands and fingers a lot and for a wide range of activities will find it easier to learn to write neatly and to do clean and careful work in school.

Children of 2 or 3 years of age usually like machines that can be switched on and off and have buttons to turn around. Surprise her, if you can, with an old radio, a clock, a light switch or some other toy that has switches and buttons on it.

Developmental activities:

- Wind-up toys become the most valuable during this age period. These toys make a sound or a movement after winding them up, which children of this age find very interesting. If you show them how to wind them up they will want to imitate you. Copying this movement succesfully requires a certain amount of muscle strength and therefore it trains muscles that would not be used in any other type of activity. This will help the child develop their manipulation skills.
- Do beading together.
- Let the child help sort dry beans or rice and allow her to clean peas or perhaps pick up crumbs.
- Create simple patterns playing with any art kit that consists of small pieces. These kinds of kits develop vision as well as manual skills.
- Let her play with bolts, screws and bigger nails that she can insert into holes. (Beware: during this age period keep doors locked from the inside and try not to keep keys in the locks.)
- Start getting familiar with jigsaw puzzles. Take a picture card and cut it in two, then later in three pieces. Ask her to put the picture back together.
- Play with play dough often.
- Let her handle various tools and teach her how to use them. She could learn about screwdrivers, a small hammer and even scissors, provided there is constant supervision.
- Give her a sheet of paper to cut up. (Use safety scissors.)
- Start to teach her how to brush her teeth. Pay attention to cleaning her teeth especially before going to bed.
- In order to be able to eat neatly one needs good manual skills. Do not let her put her hands into her food. Continuously teach her how to hold the fork and the spoon correctly and how to eat without making a mess. Show her how to use a napkin.
- Try introducing independent dressing and undressing, and doing and undoing buttons.
- The best exercise for improving fine motor skills is drawing. Start

teaching her how to draw. Give her examples that she can
copy. Choose the simplest shapes, for example, a house, a
head, a fish, a worm, etc. Divide the sheet into two: one
half is yours, the other is hers to draw on. Let her create on her own
as well. At this stage the beauty of the product doesn't count. What
the child finds the most challenging is gripping the pencil, grip and
perseverance.

• Let her paint with watercolours. This way she will learn about colours,
how to hold the brush, and she will also gain experience about mixing
colours.
• Try to stick on cut-out pictures. This is a very good task to improve
concentration. (You must teach her glue usage, too!)
• Allow her to play on a toy piano/keyboard.

Speech development

Children between two and three years of age are at different levels of
their speech development. There are some who are just starting to put
words together to form sentences, while others can recite poems and
rhymes. Shy children must be encouraged to talk. They mustn't be
mocked or laughed at for their imperfect articulation. It isn't a good
idea to ask them to pronounce certain words as this can make them feel
insecure. The parents' job at this stage is to help their children to get to
like communication. This can be achieved by listening to the child and
by talking to her a lot.

Possible speech development activities:

• Talk on a toy phone. Pretend to ring
up daddy, grandma or friends.
• Play situational games with toy
animals, dolls or puppets. Describe
the pretend situation in a few words,
then you will become one character,
and the child another, for example,
the teddy bear is going to see the dentist because he has a sore tooth;
Susie doll is going to do the shopping.
• Look at books and talk about the pictures. List the characters in the
picture and analyse the action.
• Read short stories for your child. Let her interrupt you if she has a
question or a comment.
• Teach her how to communicate with other people. She must be familiar
with the basic ways of addressing others. Use every opportunity when

there are people around. Ask her often to carry out simple tasks, for example: 'Take this to Auntie Mary and say: "Here you are!"' 'Ask daddy for the paper! Say: "Daddy, can I have the paper please?"'

- When she is given something she should say 'thank you'. This can be practised successfully through situational games.
- Remind her to say hello and goodbye.
- Make bedtime story part of the daily routine every night. It's fine if she wants to hear the same story over and over again, it only shows that she likes that story.
- Learn a few poems or rhymes by heart. (Not for showing off but for your own pleasure.) It is a mistake to think that if a 3-year-old can recite more and longer poems she will develop outstanding abilities. However, it is worth using her memorisation skill in other areas too. The point here is that she likes poems and stories and she is happy to look at books.
- Set the goal of expanding the child's vocabulary if she speaks well already, and pick your rhymes to serve this purpose.
- You should often listen to children's story CDs and music CDs together.
- Sing songs together that you already know.
- Your description of pictures in books should become more and more detailed. Adjectives and adverbs should be added to simple sentences, for example, 'The bird's flying very high in the sky.'
- Pay attention to grammatical correctness when the child can speak well. Repeat her sentence correctly but do not ask her to repeat it herself. However, if there is a recurring, deep-rooted mistake it should be pointed out to her and in this case the child should repeat the correct sentence.

Who is this funny insect?
(Talk about the picture.)

Supporting the development of thinking
To develop thinking one needs stable factual knowledge and applicable data. Combination and problem solving skills can only be built up if we have a sufficient amount of factual knowledge.

Tasks and requirements:
• The child should know the names of her body parts and should be able to point to them on her own body.
• She should be able to tell her name, age, address and the names of her siblings and parents.
• She should be familiar with the names of rooms in the house and the names of some pieces of furniture.
• The child should be able to understand the following adverbs of place: here, there, at the front and at the back. She should be familiar with the spatial positions determined by the following prepositions: next to, above, below, in front of, behind.
• She should recognise and name the following colours: red, yellow, blue, green, brown, white and black.
• To form the notion of bigger-smaller arrange buttons, discs, or blocks in a row starting from the smallest one and finishing with the biggest one. Discuss which one is the smallest/biggest.

• Sort objects according to shape, for example, cylinders, cubes and balls.
• Sort things according to colour. Make a group of red objects, another group of yellows, a third group of blues, etc.
• Create symmetric formations using geometrical forms.
• Arrange geometrical forms into asymmetric formations.
• Take two 10x15 cm sheets of cardboard and create geometrical shapes whatever way you like on one of them using buttons or discs. Ask the child to do the same on her sheet.
• Practise putting puzzles together. Take a picture or a picture card and cut it into 2-3, perhaps 4 pieces. The two of you then try to put them back together.

- Use 3 or 4 children's play cards and ask your child to pick out the identical ones. (You can also use other objects for this task.)
- Encourage the child to find a basis for grouping, for example, divide a group of animals into domestic animals and wild animals, divide a group of food into tasty ones and sour ones.
- Pick out the odd one, for example, place 3 cubes and a cylinder in front of the child. Which one is different? For example, there are 2 big dogs and a small one in a picture. Which dog is different and why?
- Try to draw her attention to the meanings of prepositions, for example, 'Put it *in* the box', 'Put it *on* the box'.
- Give the child instructions in which the place adverb is expressed by a preposition and a noun. 'Put it next to the chair', 'Hold it above your head', 'Put it under the table'.
- Use picture books to make the child aware of the notion of 'boy' and that of 'girl'.
- Bring up examples of friends and mention the words older/younger brother, and older/younger sister.
- Deal with opposite meanings while chatting or looking at books:

new-old	beautiful-ugly	closed-open
down-up	good-bad	quiet-loud
hard-soft	long-short	smart-silly
warm-cold	fat-thin	heavy-light
wide-narrow	clean-dirty	small-big

If possible, illustrate these opposite meanings in drawing as well, for example,

◻ small   ◻ big

- Play hiding an object and direct her by saying 'cold' – if she is far from it, 'warm' – if she gets closer, and 'hot' – if she is very close.
- Play driving a horse. Practise the instructions: 'Go!' and 'Stop!'
- Name parts of the day frequently, for example, 'We are doing the shopping in the morning and going for a walk in the afternoon.'
- Use the words 'today', 'yesterday' and 'tomorrow' often. It will take a long time before the child grasps the meanings of these words.
- Start introducing the meanings of the words: 'now', 'straight away' and 'later'.
- Name the meals: 'Here's your breakfast. Enjoy!'
- Start forming some concepts of mathematics.

- Take one out of a group of small objects (buttons) and leave the rest together. Ask the child which group she would choose. 'Which is more? Which is less?' Divide the buttons evenly between the two of you. 'One for me, one for you.' Let her do the distribution too. Teach her to count the numbers up to ten by practising it many times. Count your fingers. Count everything that there is more of. First only up to 3 or 5, then later she should be encouraged to continue counting, for example, count the flowers on the edge of the plate, count the dogs and hens in the picture, and the dots on the ladybird's back.
- Look at books that provide a variety of information. Do not read out what's written in them but rather have a conversation about the topic at the child's level. The child's questions will lead your explanations. When analysing a picture, mention the names of the objects, but also mention who is doing what. Listing a few adjectives will support and extend your child's vocabulary.

Enriching emotional wellbeing

A small child's emotional life gets richer through different experiences. Her own adventures and events in the family will facilitate getting to know or living through new and different emotions. Positive emotions, such as joy, surprise, calmness or love will motivate the child to repeat events that served as a source for these emotions. During her play she will pretend to live through the moments that made her feel good again and again. A successful game is enough to make a small child feel happy. Look for and, if possible, repeat those situations or events that caused the child feelings of joy and satisfaction.

- Before starting playschool try and look for places where your child can be part of a group or, at least, spend some time with a friend or cousin of her age.
- Children at the age of three do not play together, even if they are in each other's company. The fact that they are next to each other and doing their own things seems to be enough for them to be happy. Whenever your child meets playmates you should help her relate to them. Try to persuade her to swap a toy with another child, but at the same time do not let aggressive children take advantage of less assertive children all the time. If she gets hurt, defend her and teach her how to defend herself.
- By no means should you let her settle conflicts by hitting others. This could cause serious problems in playschool.

- However, do not teach her to become a victim. Teach her to defend herself against the malicious attacks from others. The best thing to do is that you 'stand behind' her in every situation and help her by solving the problems that may arise. This way, through examples, she will be able to find the right solution even when you're not around any more.
- Teach her how to apologise if she causes pain or problems to others. An apology should be a natural gesture and not a punishment for your child.
- Let's say a few words about fear. Fear first starts around the age of 8 months, when the object of fear is the separation from the mother. This is called separation anxiety. A child around 2-3 years can suddenly start complaining about a whole lot of things, where before she wasn't afraid of anything. The most common cause of fear is the dark. In darkness a child fears the unknown, abandonment and loneliness. This state is very similar to the separation anxiety they feel around 8 months. 'What I cannot see doesn't exist' – the child believes based on her experiences. She thinks that in darkness objects are not necessarily where they used to be and, possibly, there can be something else in the room, also. This anxiety is not imaginary, and therefore you should take it seriously. Do everything you can to eliminate her fear, for example, turn on a night light in her room, leave the door of her room open, check on her a good few times so that she feels she is looked after. You could sit by her bed for a while stroking and reassuring her. This way she will feel that you did not leave her alone with her worries.
- Do not ever frighten the child with something inconceivable (for example, the bogey man) and do not let anyone else do this. The worry that even you cannot protect her from these things may turn into a serious anxiety.
- Read lots of stories to your child in order to promote her feelings of joy and happiness. Choose ones that are nice and happy, for example Winnie the Pooh.
- Acquaint her with the classic stories, such as Little Red Riding Hood, The Wolf and The Seven Kids, Hansel and Gretel. Discuss these stories as they contain an element of tension. Try to relieve any conflict-induced frustration in the child.
- She should only be allowed to watch television programmes if they suit her age. The maximum time she spends in front of the TV should be half an hour daily.
- If possible, take her to see a puppet show or a theatre performance.

- Sing together a lot. Before celebrations or special days teach her songs that are connected to the celebration.
- Continue listening to children's CDs. (During the independent play periods, too.)

- Children express their feelings and thoughts through drawing. Encourage your child to draw a lot. You can arouse her interest in drawing by letting her draw on a big piece of card instead of an A4 sheet. A whole lot of things can fit in an almost child-sized piece of paper. Try to stick the big sheet on the door or the tiles in the kitchen, so that she can keep returning to it to do more work every day for a few days.
- Go to exhibitions or art shows, if you can. There is no need to explain what it is she is looking at. It is enough if she gets carried away by a nice sculpture, painting or some other work of art.
- Express your contentment at every move she makes and that you find appropriate and right, for example, 'I'm very happy that you put your toys back on the shelf.'
- To a certain extent every child goes through the so-called 'terrible two period' or the 'period of defiance'. The child's aggressive or headstrong behaviour is a nuisance, especially in shops. To be able to handle the situation requires your firm approach. However, it is essential that you do not use lying or deceiving the child as a tool to find a temporary solution. For example, instead of 'I'll buy this teddy for you tomorrow' you should say 'I know you would like this teddy a lot but I can't buy it for you now. Give him a hug and put it back on the shelf, please.' In a few situations just stop and think over why you are saying no. It can happen that you say no immediately when your child asks for a piece of chocolate but later, after getting pressurised by the child, you give in. It is better if you make a well thought out decision and then stick to it. If you are not consistent, the child will become aware that some boundaries can be broken. Then they will keep pestering you until you give in.

- Word your refusal in a way that she understands it is not her as a person you are saying no to, but something explicit. It is wrong, for example, to say this: 'I'm not buying it for you because you were bold yesterday.' The child doesn't even understand the concept of yesterday, so she cannot comprehend why her request doesn't get heard.
- Hug, stroke and express your love towards the greatest treasure of your life, whenever you can. She should wrestle and have fun with both her parents. All this will make your child feel safe.

 Aiding the development of independent play

A child around 2-3 years of age, who is being brought up in a supportive and calm environment, can play with almost everything. With any object she picks up, her imagination gets going and she starts playing. In my opinion, it is unnecessary to overwhelm the child with very expensive toys. Most of them will lose their novelty within a few days and will be thrown into the collection box anyway.

Recommended toys: a tricycle or a bicycle with stabilisers, a sand activity kit, balls (a smaller one and a bigger one), shape sorting kit (objects that can be inserted into the appropriately shaped holes), play dough (a multi-coloured set and another single-colour one), a good size car for loading and unloading things, a beading kit, children's play cards, a Lego set, a stamper kit, a couple of small cars, dolls and a few plastic animals.

When choosing toys, try to pick ones that are really good for playing with and not ones that only look good.

Take into consideration the child's habits and interests, but sometimes it is useful to get something that will be new to her. Try not to buy toy swords, rifles and guns, as these are not suitable for any other game but aggressive play. Toy soldiers and horses offer a chance for a more creative game, but if your child doesn't ask for them it is best not to buy these toys, either.

Do not send her off to play saying: 'Now, go and play something!' For the period of independent play recommend an alternative from the collection of toys to your child, for example, 'Build a home for the Lego people or a stable for the horses out of building blocks. Play racing with the cars. Build a tunnel over the toy train. Put the doggy to bed. Take the doll for a walk. Make a mummy snail, a daddy snail, and a baby snail out of play dough. Do some stamping and colour it in. Blow bubbles. Listen to music and do some drumming. Comb Susie doll's hair. Make a nice drawing for daddy.'

I'm not going to extend this list of possibilities. You should make a suggestion according to your own stock of toys. If she is reluctant to play on her own give her a hand by starting off together, then leave her.

Here are a few words about situations where you are supposed to direct the play of a number of children around the same age.

Stay at home mums often help each other by minding each other's children while they catch up on things they can't do with their children. It isn't easy to look after 2-3 children, especially if they are unable to play together or if they spend their time crying for toys that the other child has.

It is advisable that you join them and initiate an enjoyable game or activity. You should never offer alternatives for joint play, for example, 'What shall we play? Shopping or doctors?' It is almost certain that each of them will want something different. Instead of that introduce the new game like this: 'Let's play shopping. I will be the shopkeeper and you will be the customers.' Always choose a game in which every child can take part. When the game is over start telling a story or sing songs.

Other ideas for joint play: pretend family with dolls, doctors, shopping, travelling, handymen, visiting the zoo, vets, feeding animals, building site, etc.

Sets of activities for children aged 24-36 months

TASK OF THE MONTH
To practise washing hands thoroughly.
Every day, before and after each session, wash hands using soap.

1st week

Monday	• Make a cake out of play dough. Decorate it with seeds then give it to the child's favourite toy as a present.
Tuesday	• Do exercises: jump up and down, lift your arms and legs from a lying position, cycle with your legs in the air. Pretend you are on a walk in the woods and you have to go across a narrow plank: stretch two pieces of wool on the carpet and walk between them.
Wednesday	• Check how she knows the objects in her surroundings using picture books. If she can talk, ask her: 'What's this?' and if she cannot speak yet, ask her: 'Where's the brush?'
Thursday	• Let her practise putting on her underwear and socks by herself.
Friday	• Do a colour recognition activity. Colour with red, yellow and blue. Look at magazine pictures of objects and clothes in various colours.

2nd week

Monday	• Give her objects with a screw-on top to play with.
Tuesday	• Talk on a toy phone.
Wednesday	• Listen to music and dance to it.
Thursday	• Build very tall towers. Teach her that she should put the bigger pieces at the bottom as a foundation and that she should use smaller and smaller blocks towards the top.
Friday	• Play: 'This little piggy'. Name her fingers.

3rd week

Monday	• Pick out the cubes, the cylinders and the cones out of 10-15 building blocks. Place them in different groups.
Tuesday	• Look at animals living in far away lands (for example, chimpanzees, lions, elephants, giraffes) in a picture book and name them.  
Wednesday	• Play hide and seek: you hide and ask the child to find you by listening to your voice. Then ask *her* to hide.
Thursday	• Do some colouring in a colouring book with coloured pencils and crayons.
Friday	• When outdoors, arrange stones and sticks into various formations.

4th week

Monday	• Give her a bolt and a nut so that she can practise her dexterity.
Tuesday	• Play situational games with dolls and toy animals. Take them for an outing. Prepare a picnic and prepare some food for the toy animals as well. Discuss which animal eats what.
Wednesday	• Play hiding objects: hide a good size object in such a way that you leave a small part of it sticking out of the drawer, or from under the bed or curtain. Tell her where it is. (This is good practice for adverbs of place and prepositions.)
Thursday	• Watch the sky while out walking. Notice the birds and clouds and show her the sun.
Friday	• Tell her a short story about her own life.

TASK OF THE MONTH
To do daily exercises and play ball.

1st week

Monday	• Look at her baby photos. Name people in the pictures you know. Let her hold the pictures but do not let her crush them.
Tuesday	• To improve her manual skills string buttons on a fishing line. Do not use beads for the first time as with beads the child has to push the line through a thick surface.
Wednesday	• Teach her to put on, button up, take off and perhaps fold her shirt or blouse. Do not rush her.
Thursday	• Roll worms out of play dough. Let her slice them with a toy knife.
Friday	• Look at flowers during your walk. Smell them, pick them and make a small bouquet. Show her again where to hold them when picking them.

2nd week

Monday	• Practise the primary colours: red, yellow and blue. Colour flowers and objects red, yellow and blue. Use discs or buttons to sort red and blue apart.
Tuesday	• Pay attention to the right grip of the spoon and the fork. Feed the toy animals and the dolls.
Wednesday	• Make a house and for the roof place a book on top. Then you can build another floor on it. Make beds out of small boxes for the toys to rest in.
Thursday	• Give her safety scissors and some paper so she can cut away. The rubbish can be collected in a 'rubbish truck'. Stick the cut outs on a sheet to form a picture.
Friday	• Practise following instructions, for example, 'Take this to daddy and say: "Here you are"', 'Bring me the dustpan'

3rd week

Monday	• Try counting her fingers on one hand from 1 to 5. Name the fingers.
Tuesday	• Draw and scribble with sticks in sand or on the ground. 
Wednesday	• Drive a horse. Put a scarf on her around her waist and practise: 'Go, … stop!' You should become the horse after a while, so she can practise saying the words too.
Thursday	• Do exercises: teach her to walk club-footed, in squatting, while stretching up high, and also to do a forward tumble, and lean backwards.
Friday	• Do shape recognition with three different shapes.

4th week

Monday	• Practise the body parts. 'Where shall I tie the ribbon? Around your elbow, your ankle, or your forehead? Where's your elbow?', etc.
Tuesday	• Play with wool. Cut off long and short pieces. Separate the long ones from the short ones. Say and show: short, long. Show her how to tie them around something.
Wednesday	• Listen to music and try to clap to the rhythm – help the child.
Thursday	• Practise sorting blue and yellow apart using rectangle cut-outs of coloured sheets. Stick them on a sheet making a picture while practising place adverbs: below, above, next to, between.
Friday	• Visit the zoo or a museum. Go to a place where the child hasn't been yet.

TASK OF THE MONTH
To practise saying colours.
Colour in a colouring book every day but use three colours only,
for example, yellow-red-green, red-blue-yellow.

1st week

Monday	• Give her a pencil. Draw long straight lines. Draw a snake. Scribble on the page without lifting up the pencil for a long time.
Tuesday	• Arrange buttons or discs on a 10x15 cm sheet to make definite formations. Ask the child to make the same formation on her sheet.
Wednesday	• Play shape recognition using four or more objects.
Thursday	• Practise putting on and taking off her trousers. Trousers with an elasticated waist are easier to put on and off.
Friday	• Place cups and cubes into and on top of each other. Put the smaller ones on top of the bigger ones. Put them the other way and build a tower.

2nd week

Monday	• Build a multi-storey building again. Make a door and a window on the first floor or just make three sides to it. Put animals on the first floor and the second floor too.
Tuesday	• Play: who can get to the TV, washing machine, fridge, DVD player or the night light before the other person? Practise names of household equipment.
Wednesday	• Look at people in a picture book. Name what they are doing.
Thursday	• Do exercises: learn how to march to a rhyme or a made up song. Lift your legs and arms a couple of times while lying on your back.
Friday	• Let her cut with safety scissors. Stick the pieces she cut out on a sheet. Practise the words: below, above, between and next to, with their meanings.

3rd week

Monday	• Get to know the colour green. Cut out various shapes, for example, a moon shape, birds and flowers of red, green and yellow sheets. Sort them into groups according to colour or shape. Stick them on a blank sheet using one of the groups you made earlier.
Tuesday	• Imitate animal sounds, for example, a duck, a snake, a lion and a monkey. Try to imitate their movements too.
Wednesday	• Turn on the radio. Make it play quietly first, and then gradually make it louder. Say: 'quiet, loud'. You should talk quietly/loudly, too: your ears will become the balance control button.
Thursday	• Play a situation game. Take the animals and dolls to visit a friend. Place a table (a box), a tablecloth (a napkin), some flowers in a vase (small medicine bottle), small plates and spoons (matchsticks can be used for these) in front of them. Talk about what you are going to serve and to whom.
Friday	• Read a story. Learn a short poem.

4th week

Monday	• Play with play dough. Make hedgehogs (a ball of dough with half matchsticks stuck in it), trees (a dough cylinder with matchsticks as branches) and snakes out of the play dough. Play with these objects.
Tuesday	• Go to some water and let her throw stones in it. Show her the technique of throwing.
Wednesday	• Get an old clock that doesn't work any more and allow her to play with winding it. Take off the removable parts, and then put them back. Play handyman.
Thursday	• Colour with crayons. Use the colours blue, red, yellow, green and brown in a colouring book.
Friday	• Read her a short story. Make a drawing of the characters.

TASK OF THE MONTH
To listen to children's songs on a CD every day.

1st week

Monday	• Put colourful plastic beads in a jar. Put the lid on and let the child play with it. (Supervised.)
Tuesday	• Take the two 10x15 cm cardboard sheets that you used before and create formations on them.
Wednesday	• Learn a few words with opposite meanings: open – closed, thin – fat, short – tall and narrow – wide. Draw pictures in which the opposite meanings can be seen clearly.
Thursday	• Look at books with pictures of fruit and vegetables in them. Name these.
Friday	• Trace people's eyes and hands in magazine pictures and also trace pictures of round and angular objects. Practise gripping the pencil correctly.

2nd week

Monday	• Make a row of building blocks and a row of toy cars. Start with the biggest one and finish with the smallest. Use at least 5-6 pieces.
Tuesday	• Teach her how to water plants. Put a little water in the can and let her practise pouring out the water.
Wednesday	• Play ball: roll it and try to catch it.
Thursday	• Play with play dough: roll out 2 or 3 flat plates using a pencil as a rolling pin and make round balls too to put on the plates. Practise: 'flat-round'.
Friday	• Listen to music. Clap the rhythm of the songs.

3rd week

Monday	• Review the concepts of warm and cold in her bath using a cup of water, like you did before. Show her what lukewarm is like. While showing the full cup say: 'It's heavy, because it's full.' While showing the other cup say: 'It's light, because it's empty.'
Tuesday	• Place a plastic plate on her open palm with her arm outstretched and put a few pieces of food on it. She can be the waitress and take the food to certain places. She should try to balance the plate.
Wednesday	• Empty the kitchen cupboard together. Name the objects and explain what each of them is used for. Let her see a grater, a grinder, a squeezer, a pan and a saucepan. Allow her to find the right size lids.
Thursday	• Pull out a bunch of grass together outside. Show her a bush, and put her up on a smaller tree.
Friday	• Make colour groups (blue, red and yellow) using discs and building blocks. Check her knowledge.

4th week

Monday	• Do exercises: teach her how to do a wheelbarrow, how to jump with her feet together and how to walk on her hands and knees.
Tuesday	• Imitate each other's movements: put your hands on your head, in front of your eyes; stand on one leg; pull your own ears forward with your hands; etc.
Wednesday	• Play hiding an object, then hide and seek.
Thursday	• Practise walking to the beat. Make a 'train' with you at the front. Sing a song about a train. The runaway train came down the track and she blew, The runaway train came down the track and she blew, The runaway train came down the track, her whistle wide and her throttle back, And she blew, blew, blew, blew, blew. Coordinate both of your steps so the train doesn't shake about.
Friday	• Go to a place that the child doesn't know very well. Encourage her to communicate with grown-ups you know.

TASK OF THE MONTH
To learn 1-3 nursery rhyme(s).
Recite the chosen rhyme(s) a few times every day.

1st week

Monday	• Put a few raisins in a box that has a small opening, so the child's hand doesn't fit through. This way she cannot open the box, but if she tilts it or turns it upside down the goodies will fall out. Let her keep experimenting and practising.
Tuesday	• Give her safety scissors and let her try cutting.
Wednesday	• Let her try out tools in and around the house. Show the child how to use a hoe, a rake, a watering can or a hammer and the pliers. Repeat the names of these objects a few times. Ask her to hand you this one or that one. (Make sure she is safe.)
Thursday	• Play with play dough. Roll snakes and roll them up to become snails. The snails could talk about the weather.
Friday	• Play ball. Roll it, and teach her how to bounce it and throw it up. (Naturally, she won't be able to catch it yet.)

2nd week

Monday	• Build a building with a round ground-plan. Insert wedges between the angular blocks to make the building round.
Tuesday	• Cut a postcard in half and show her how to put the two halves back together. Let the child try it on her own. You can cut up 2 or 3 postcards, too.
Wednesday	• Practise describing positions with plastic animals. Use the most common prepositions: between, next to, in front of and behind.
Thursday	• Pick up a few leaves while out walking. Press them at home. Try crushing the dry leaves and listen to the sound they make. Break a dry stick and say: 'crack and groan'.
Friday	• Listen to music and march to the beat. (Use children's songs.)

3rd week

Monday	• Do exercises. Teach her to do a forward tumble, to skip (on two legs and on one leg), to run and to stop.
Tuesday	• Place plastic nails, bolts and a board with holes in it in front of her to play with. Lift the board and help with screwing the nuts on the bolts. (Keep her supervised.)
Wednesday	• Teach her how to put on and take off her shoes. Teach the first, basic part of tying shoelaces or using Velcro straps (do not teach forming two loops yet.)
Thursday	• Experiment with arranging matchsticks. You can build formations and let the child play with them freely.
Friday	• Imitate animal sounds and guess the animal.

4th week

Monday	• Act out a short scene using puppets. (If you have no puppets, plastic animals will do.) The topic should be: getting up, getting washed and getting dressed in the morning.
Tuesday	• Draw animals using simple lines.
Wednesday	• Play with your fingers and name them. Draw small human figures on her index fingers.
Thursday	• Put a plastic container with a narrow opening in her bath, so she can sprinkle the water out of it and make air bubbles.
Friday	• Watch vehicles while out walking. Name what you see.

TASK OF THE MONTH
To establish rules around toilet usage.
Children should be taught how to use toilet paper even after
doing a wee! To practise flushing the loo and washing hands.

1st week

Monday	• Place at least four smaller and bigger objects (which can be put into each other) in front of her. Encourage her to put them together.
Tuesday	• Do a shape recognition exercise. She should be able to do it with three different shapes. Increase the number of the shapes. Make the exercise harder by involving irregular shaped objects.
Wednesday	• Listen to music and bang to the rhythm on a bed or a table.
Thursday	• Collect interesting looking leaves, seeds and nuts outdoors (horse chestnut when it is in season, etc).
Friday	• Draw pieces of thread (long and short lines) and practise saying: 'long… short'. Draw coloured beads on the threads. Colour them in with circular movements.

2nd week

Monday	• Do exercises: imitate animal movements. Stretch out and curl up like a snake; crawl like a spider; jump like a frog, etc.
Tuesday	• String beads on fishing line. (Choose big beads with big holes in them.)
Wednesday	• Look at a picture of a forest in a book and name the animals that live there (for example, the fox, the hedgehog, the owl). Talk about their way of life and what they eat.
Thursday	• Use building blocks to build flat formations and ask your child to build the same formations.
Friday	• Get a bag of raisins and pick out 6-8 pieces. Divide them between you: one for me, one for you. Count how many you got each. Divide them in other ways. Practise this a few times.

3rd week

Monday	• Ask her to put together the two halves of a postcard that you had cut up. (Do not cut vertically but diagonally.)
Tuesday	• Give the child a broken clock to play with.
Wednesday	• Take the child to an exhibition or a museum.
Thursday	• Act out a short scene using puppets. Take a topic from the child's life. Let her have one of the puppets to move it and make it talk.
Friday	• Show her spices in the kitchen, for example, salt, paprika, cinnamon, cumin, cloves, pepper. Smell and taste them. Let her stick some of them into play dough.

4th week

Monday	• Get the child to learn her name, the names of her mother and father and her address.
Tuesday	• Play hiding an object and say 'cold' if she is faraway, say 'warm' if she is closer, and say 'hot' if she is close. If she doesn't understand, play it differently: leave a small part of the object out when hiding it, so it is visible.
Wednesday	• Dance to some music.
Thursday	• Play a hand slapping game. One of you holds out their hands, palms up. The other has to put their palms onto the other's palms. The person whose hands are on the top has to pull their hands away very fast when the other person tries to hit them.
Friday	• Look at pictures of water animals (sharks, whales, starfish, jellyfish, fishes). Name them. 

TASK OF THE MONTH
**To improvise a scene with the help of two toy animals or dolls.
Choose a different topic every day.**

1st week

Monday	• Draw trees, bushes and flowers.
Tuesday	• Get to know the colours black and white. On a checked sheet leave some of the squares white, and colour the rest black.
Wednesday	• Count the child's fingers up to five. Play with a small object: which hand is it hiding in?
Thursday	• Sort some change. The child should pick out the 10 cent coins. (Wash hands afterwards.)
Friday	• Put 3-4 cards out of a children's pack on the table and see if there are any identical ones.

2nd week

Monday	• Copy each other's movements: stand on one leg, squat down, stand on hands and knees, make faces.
Tuesday	• If it's nice outside, pick some colourful flowers and watch the butterflies and small insects.
Wednesday	• Place a book on the child's head to balance. It is enough if she just stands with it. She can try walking with a pillow on the top of her head.
Thursday	• Go to the bathroom and ask the child about the names of things. She should know the words for the soap, the towel, the sponge, the nailbrush, the toothbrush, the toothpaste, etc. Discuss what they are used for.
Friday	• Teach her how to button her shirt, how to dress herself, how to undress, how to put her clothes down nicely.

3rd week

Monday	• If you have a friend who can play an instrument, visit them. Ask them to play for you.
Tuesday	• Do a shape recognition exercise tailored to the child's knowledge.
Wednesday	• Review the colours by looking at a magazine. 'Which is red, yellow, green, brown, blue, white, black?' Or: 'What colour is this?'
Thursday	• Do exercises: put her on a bar so that she hangs upside down for a while. (Make sure she is safe in case she falls.) Jump up from squatting, circle with your arms, lean your body forward a few times.
Friday	• Learn a short rhyme by heart.

4th week

Monday	• Play hiding an object and, if possible, use the cold-warm-hot instructions.
Tuesday	• Listen to music and play conductors to the rhythm.
Wednesday	• Place discs or buttons on the 10x15 cm cardboard sheet that you have used a few times before and ask the child to copy you. Let *her* give *you* tasks, too. 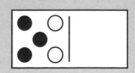 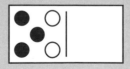
Thursday	• Talk on behalf of toy animals or puppets. The topic can be shopping.
Friday	• Play with play dough. Roll the dough until it's as thick as your finger using a pencil. Cut off the edges with a knife. Decorate it with dry flowers, seeds, feathers or some other small objects.

TASK OF THE MONTH
To practise dressing independently.

1st week

Monday	• Draw a house, a fence, a flower and a person together.
Tuesday	• Trace around shapes on coloured paper. (You can make simple shapes: a circle, a square, a car, a flower, a bird etc.) Cut them out. You can make a beautiful picture by sticking on 4-5 birds of different colours.
Wednesday	• Do exercises: lie down and lift your legs and arms, cycle with your legs, and be a wheelbarrow.
Thursday	• Knock together objects of various materials (for example, plastic, metal, wood). Name these materials.
Friday	• Watch vehicles during your walk. Talk about how many people are travelling in them (few or many).

2nd week

Monday	• During the day count everything that's more than one. (Do not choose more than five objects.) Count the plates, the spoons, the napkins, the chairs, etc.
Tuesday	• Tidy the child's wardrobe together. Show her how to fold different articles of clothing.
Wednesday	• Learn some rhymes or poems.
Thursday	• Play with children's play cards. Put all of them out on the table and look for pairs.
Friday	• Play with play dough: make a centipede and make a 'centinose' (a creature with a hundred noses). For the centipede roll a worm, then stick lots of halved matchsticks into it. For the centinose use 2 balls of dough. Make lots of tiny noses in one of them (this will be the head) by pinching it many times.

3rd week

Monday	• Do beading. Try to create the three-colour pattern again.
Tuesday	• Listen to music. Keep repeating the same set of movements, which consists of a few pieces, to the same music.
Wednesday	• Look at books with pictures of domestic animals. Name them and imitate the sounds they make.
Thursday	• Cut up a postcard or a magazine picture into 2-3-4 pieces. Let the child try to put the pieces back together.
Friday	• Practise tying a knot on a ribbon. Try to make a bow as well.

4th week

Monday	• Build a house with a few rooms using wooden blocks. It shouldn't have more than 2 floors. Place small toys in the rooms that would indicate what the rooms are used for. Play with it.
Tuesday	• Play with puppets. The topic should be: getting cleaned up.
Wednesday	• Acquaint your child with painting. Do not let her paint with more than two colours initially. Teach her how to dip the brush in the paint, how to draw it on the side of the dish and how to hold it.
Thursday	• Look at magazines. Encourage her to talk about what she sees.
Friday	• Play ball: teach her how to bounce it on the ground and how to catch it. Try to throw a smaller ball into a bucket.

TASK OF THE MONTH
To make one or two simple drawings every day
(a head, a stick man, a ball, a hammer, a mushroom,
an ice cream cone etc.).

1st week

Monday	• Play with an art set that has small colourful pieces in it for creating patterns. If you do not have such a kit, use buttons or discs to make patterns. Try to make the three-colour pattern again.
Tuesday	• Look at a book with pictures of buildings in it. Use the following words: hut, cottage, palace and castle.
Wednesday	• Practise her personal details. Her name, her father's name, her mother's name, the name(s) of her sibling(s), her address and her age.
Thursday	• Visit friends. Encourage her to address the grown-ups whom she knows, and to ask them for things or communicate with them. Help her to word her message.
Friday	• Make a pattern using wooden blocks. Then ask the child to make the same pattern.

2nd week

Monday	• Wrestle; mess about a bit. Cuddle and hug her; play freely together.
Tuesday	• Count the fingers up to five. Put out buttons or discs for the child to try and count them.
Wednesday	• Assess how well the child knows the parts of the day. It isn't a problem if she cannot tell the difference yet. Start forming the concept by talking about the night.
Thursday	• Give instructions to the child. Watch how sure she is when she is trying to find her way in the rooms of the house and how much she understands place adverbs.
Friday	• Put out a few sets of three children's playcards in which two cards are identical. Ask the child to pick out the odd ones.

3rd week

Monday	• Depict the following opposing concepts by drawing objects and people: small-big, round-angular, crying-laughing, wide-narrow, and long-short.
Tuesday	• Look at different types of fruit in a book. Group them according to tastes (sweet or sour) and according to liking ('I like it' or 'I don't like it').
Wednesday	• Play with puppets. Make the puppets talk about the morning, then let the child pick a topic.

Thursday	• Watch butterflies, bugs and insects during your walk.
Friday	• Listen to music. Dance and be merry.

4th week

Monday	• Play on a toy phone. Call daddy and grandma.
Tuesday	• Put wooden blocks on top of each other until the tower is very high.
Wednesday	• Stick magazine cut-outs on a blank sheet. Help her with cutting and gluing.
Thursday	• Do exercises. March to music and do arm exercises and bending. Move your fingers around.
Friday	• Create a very simple rhythm by tapping a pencil 3-4 times. Ask the child to tap the same rhythm.

TASK OF THE MONTH
To practise communicating with strangers or other grown-ups (that you know and feel comfortable with).
Give her tasks to buy things in a shop and take her to the playground.

1st week

Monday	• Practise lacing up shoes and tying a knot.
Tuesday	• Play ball. Kick and throw it to each other. Try to kick the ball into the goal. (A good size box or a crate will do.)
Wednesday	• Make a UFO and an alien out of play dough. Your imagination will lead the way.
Thursday	• Practise the child's personal details. Her name, her father's name, her mother's name, the name(s) of her sibling(s), her address and her age. She can try and introduce herself with a handshake.
Friday	• Fold a sheet into 4 parts, fold back the free ends, cut off the centre and you will have a funnel. Let her fill it with water in the bath.

2nd week

Monday	• Stick pressed leaves on a sheet.
Tuesday	• Do a shape recognition exercise.
Wednesday	• Let her paint with 2-3 colours. Draw three triangles on a sheet. Ask her to fill two of them with the same colour.
Thursday	• Invite a child of a similar age over and watch how your child behaves. Help her make friends.
Friday	• Build something that your child suggests. You can also make a slope as an addition where cars and animals can slide down.

3rd week

Monday	• Give her safety scissors to do some cutting. Start practising how to follow a line.
Tuesday	• Do exercises. When you clap, the child should stop and squat down. Do forward tumbles, and roll on the floor.
Wednesday	• Listen to music. Pick a children's song that she knows well. Sing along with the radio or a CD.
Thursday	• Organise a date where she can play with children.
Friday	• Learn a short poem by heart.

4th week

Monday	• Spend a bit more time on shopping. Show the child various items, for example, washing powder, milk, soap, salami, bread or juice. Ask her if she knows what they are called.
Tuesday	• Look at photographs. Name the family members in the pictures. Talk about who is whose mother and father, and who is whose child.
Wednesday	• Practise the body parts. Get a toy animal and make it jump from one body part to another on the child. Ask her where the bunny is.
Thursday	• Put together 3-4 pieces of a cut-up picture. (Puzzle)
Friday	• Play with cards. Pull cards and sort them into pairs. 

TASK OF THE MONTH
To assess the child's level of development.

Underline what applies to your child.

1st week

Monday	• Independent dressing
	    – age appropriate
	    – needs great help
	    – dependent

Tuesday	• Colour recognition
	(red, blue, yellow, green, brown, white and black)
	    – recognises all listed colours
	    – recognises a few colours
	    – unable to recognise colours

Wednesday	• Familiarity with personal details
	(name, age, address, father's name, mother's name, name(s) of sibling(s))
	    – familiar with all data
	    – familiar with some of the data
	    – only knows her name

Thursday	• Understanding of instructions ('Give it to me', 'Come here', 'Put it on the table', 'Go to the room', 'Bring your teddy here').
	    – understands everything and carries out requests
	    – understands everything but doesn't always carry out requests
	    – shows no reaction to requests

Friday	• Shape recognition (regular and irregular shapes)
	    – able to insert any shaped object into the appropriate slot
	    – finds the right slot by trial and error
	    – no patience for this exercise

Note

....

....

....

....

2nd week

Monday	• Knowledge of rhymes and poems – can recite familiar rhymes and poems without mistakes – makes mistakes when reciting poems – unable to recite rhymes or poems
Tuesday	• Construction play – likes building for a long time – puts the blocks on each other randomly for a short period – doesn't like building
Wednesday	• Familiarity with domestic animals and the sounds they make – can name the animals and imitates their sounds – recognises the animals by their name and imitates the sounds they make – mixes up the animals and their sounds
Thursday	• Playing ball and kicking – rolls, throws and kicks back the ball when rolled to her – rolls and kicks the stationary ball – kicking is difficult for the child
Friday	• Independent feeding – eats and drinks unassisted and neatly – eats and drinks independently but drops food on her clothing and the table – the child needs to be fed by an adult

Note

....
....
....
....
....
....
....
....
....

Monday	• Knowledge of numbers
	    – counts three objects easily
	    – only knows one and two
	    – has no knowledge of quantity

Tuesday	• Doing physical exercises
	    – copies movements well
	    – unable to copy movements independently
	    – doesn't do exercises

Wednesday	• Familiarity with locality
	('Lead me to the shop and tell me what we see')
	    – has a good sense of direction and is familiar with her surroundings
	    – would get lost on her own walking on a familiar path
	    – does not have a good sense of direction

Thursday	• Puzzle
	    – able to put together a 4-piece picture
	    – able to put together a 2-piece picture
	    – not interested in this activity

Friday	• Communication with strangers and familiar people
	    – starts a conversation with anyone
	    – communicates with familiar people only
	    – too shy to talk to people other than family members

Note

4th week

Monday	• Playing with play dough
	   – likes playing and tries to form figures
	   – shapes play dough randomly
	   – does not engage in the activity

Tuesday	• Story telling – (ask her not to interrupt this time)
	   – listens to a short story with patience
	   – shows interest in the story but interrupts with
	     her questions and comments
	   – listening to a tale does not hold her interest

Wednesday	• Drawing, colouring
	   – basic shapes appear in her drawings
	   – scribbles
	   – doesn't engage in drawing

Thursday	• Looking at books – picture analysis
	   – finds pleasure in looking at books and chats about
	     what she sees
	   – looks at books for a short while, does not talk about
	     the pictures independently but answers questions
	   – shows no interest in this activity

Friday	• Music, dance
	   – likes songs and dancing
	   – finds pleasure in listening to music but does not dance
	     herself
	   – not interested in music

Note

This assessment form was made only so that you can form a more realistic picture of your child. By no means should you draw far-reaching conclusions from the results.

There is one thing you should pay attention to if you had to choose the 3rd option a lot. This will tell you that you should spend more time with your child and on joint play activities. Tasks and actions carried out together will direct her interest and improve her concentration skills and determination.

It is important that you never tell the child off if she is not up for an activity. Try to find out what areas the child likes and attempt to weave the less favourable activities into those, for example, the child likes playing with play dough but she is not keen on counting. In this case make dough balls and count those.

Don't forget, most of the time a series of changes in quantity (repetition, practice) turn into a change in quality (suddenly she knows something she did not know before).

During the next few months try to strengthen those areas where you are not happy with your child's results. Your play should not be based on a result-centered learning regime, but should be filled with imaginative and creative ideas.

Enjoy and have fun!

Activity images used for children aged 3-6 years

 Mathematical tasks

 Environmental tasks

 Speech exercises

 Dexterity tasks

 Activities to aid emotional wellbeing

 Movement development exercises

 Practice exercises

 Games for independent play

 Family games

 Rules of behaviour

 Music therapy activities

 Activities to improve thinking or memory skills

 Safety advice

Development of children aged 3-6 years

The intellectual development of children gradually unfolds between the ages of 3 and 6 years. New elements appear in their thinking, their observation skills become more exact, and they are continuously looking for explanations for the phenomena of the world. During this time, after the period of the 'what's this?' question, there comes the 'why?' period. It is important that the parents or grown-ups have enough patience to answer all the questions. Even if it seems that the child doesn't understand the answer, you should try to explain the essence of the matter simply. It is useless to engage yourself into lengthy explanations. Also, you shouldn't give answers that are untrue. If you don't know something, you should consult books or the internet and get back to the question, even after a few days, and give an explanation then. It's okay to tell the child that you do not know the answer, and make a promise that you will find out. This approach is educational in itself as you are suggesting to your child that you cannot know everything, but what you can do is find a way to look things up. This way the child will become interested and open. You should involve the child in the research, if possible. You can look through books or browse the internet together.

Children at 3-6 years are very open to everything and, therefore, they should get a multi-level developmental support within their home. It is a real pleasure for the parent to see their child making progress and becoming more interested in the world around them and gaining knowledge of new things. Joint play or activities are a great help for the parent, as during these activities they can discover which areas are the ones where the child is doing well, and at the same time, they will find out which areas need support. By carrying out joint activities children become self-confident and balanced as they get the parental attention they need a lot of during this age period.

Developmental activities
for children aged 3-4 years

September

Personal details

At this age it is expected that the child knows their own personal details. Make a passport for the child. It can be bigger than the one grown-ups have, it can be a book with a few pages. You can use either the mother's or the father's passport as a sample. The child can draw their self portrait on it.

While it's being made you can practise the most important pieces of data, such as their name, their age, their sex, their address, their father's name, their mother's name and their parents' occupations.

Later, you can make further pages, which can be attached to the book, with drawings of the family members and a picture of the house where you live. Make fingerprints as well with the help of an inkpad. The successfully prepared passport can be put in the child's bag and they can carry it with them at all times, if they like.

Talk about families of people you know

Who are the father, the mother and what are their names? Explain that grandmothers are the mothers and grandfathers are the fathers of the parents. Draw a family tree of your own family with the child:

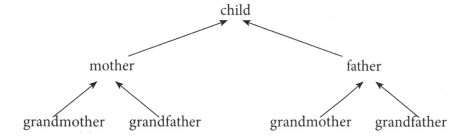

If your child is not interested in drawing, just talk about these things a few times.

The world of colours

Practising colours was part of the suggested activities a couple of times before. Now, as a review, draw in colouring pencils or paint a nice summery picture together. You should do most of the drawing so that the child's main task is the colouring.

You can check the application of all known colours by recalling a pool scene, or a walk in the woods or in the fields.

The following colours should appear in the picture: red, yellow, blue, green, brown, white and black. It is a great achievement if the child recognises other colours besides these ones.

October

Body parts in detail
You have been dealing with names of the body parts. It is time to test the child's knowledge.
Place a big piece of wrapping paper on the floor and lay the child on it. Trace around their body. Ask them to name or to point to the head, the trunk (the chest, the tummy), the arms and the legs.
Help them draw the eyes, the mouth, the ears, the nose, the hair and the nails. Allow the child to lead the work. (Ask them about the position of the elbows, the wrists, the knees, the ankles and the shoulders.)
You can paint or colour the picture together.
If you cannot finish the project by the end of the day, cut it out and stick it on the door or the tiles in the kitchen so that the child can work on it at a later stage. It will be great fun to draw or to stick on a hat, earrings, a tie or a necklace as an addition.

Counting, grouping
To practise mathematics you will need a lot of (approx. 15-20) buttons.
Ask the child to put one aside then ask them: 'Which group would you like to play with?'
They should understand the relationship between one and more.
Pick five buttons so that each is a different size. Ask the child to arrange them according to size.
Ask them to pick out, for example, the white ones. They should also count how many of them there are.
Make a group of the ones with four holes in them or other groups of buttons that are different from the rest in a small feature.
Arrange the buttons in groups of three. Your child should do the same.

Developing a sense of rhythm
Sing a few short songs together. Ask your child to clap along. Listen to a children's musical CD; ask your child to be a drummer and beat along to the rhythm with their hands or a pencil.

Names of days

Repeat a few times and learn the names of the days as a sequence. Show them a calendar with the seven days of the week in a page. Count how many days make a week. Draw a bed, a smiling sun or some other image on Saturday and Sunday to indicate that you don't have to work and you can rest on these days.

Learn this rhyme by heart:

> 'Monday alone,
> Tuesday together,
> Wednesday we walk
> When it's fine weather.
> Thursday we kiss,
> Friday we cry,
> Saturday hours
> Seem almost to fly.
> But of all the days in the week, we will call
> Sunday, the rest day, the best day of all.'

Get your child to practise the days of the week a number of times during the month.

Foundation of the concept of even numbers

What do we have two of? Which of our body parts are in pairs? You can use the drawing you made in the previous month to do this task.

Why is it bad if you have only one of the paired body parts? Your child should cover one of their eyes and ears. Now you show them a picture on the side of the covered eye and whisper in their covered ear.

Make them unwrap something with one hand. Ask them to jump on one leg.

Find a pair for a few chosen objects (for example, two combs, two cups, two pencils).

Practise doing puzzles

Find out how many pieces of a puzzle your child can put together.

To be able to finish a 5 or 6 piece puzzle is very good.

For this activity you can use a postcard that you had cut into pieces and give it to your child as a challenge.

December

A month of holidays – preparing for Christmas
Create a fairy tale type atmosphere while waiting for Christmas.
Children of this age find the celebration very exciting. Do make time for doing preparations. Only a child can experience this period as a magical time.
Christmas offers a fantastic opportunity to enhance your child's emotional life.
Tell your child about the origins of this celebration, the birth of Jesus. If you are not a religious person, it is still a good idea to visit a church on one of the days during the Christmas period.
Tell your child stories about Jesus.
Sing Christmas songs together.
For example:
'Jingle bells'; 'Rudolph the Red-nose Reindeer'; 'Silent night', etc.
Ask them to draw a picture of what they would like to get for Christmas.
Involve them in the Christmas preparations: baking cakes, folding napkins, decorating the tree, making Christmas cards.
During the holidays play together with the new toys.
Wrestle, go for walks and relax together.
Spend as much time as possible with your child, as this is the chance to enjoy yourselves together in peace.

What do people use for travelling?
Talk to your child about the different types of vehicles people use for travelling, for instance, vehicles that can go on water, on land or in the air. Tell them that the following game involves three bodily positions or movements – one for water, air and land.

'If you hear me saying the name of a water vehicle, lie down on your tummy. If I say the name of a land vehicle, sit down, and if I say the name of an air vehicle, stay standing and wave your arms as if you were flying: train, helicopter, motorboat, truck, cargo boat, aeroplane, underground train, spaceship, hydrofoil, submarine, camel.'

Talk about the vehicles they don't know.

(It is a good idea to play this game at least twice during the month.)

Make a picture in which the underground goes under the ground, above it the tram goes, and a helicopter is flying in the air. On another sheet draw a submarine diving under the water, a boat gliding over the water, and an aeroplane carrying passengers flying in the air. You can use books to help you with the drawings or you could also cut out and stick on magazine pictures.

January

Winter activities

Go over the names of the seasons and discuss their differences.

Draw a wintry picture together and talk about the following topics:

'Why do we draw the winter trees bare?' (Talk about the difference between evergreen 'coniferous' and deciduous trees.)

When drawing a snowman use the words: big – smaller – the smallest.

Discuss why we cannot see certain animals this time of the year. (They are hiding or hibernating, or they have moved to warmer countries.)

'How do animals protect themselves against the cold?' (They grow thicker fur or more hair, they move into secret hollows, they move less.)

'How do people dress in the winter time?' Dress a doll or teddy in warm winter clothes and take it for a walk.

Experiment with water. Pour some water into a plastic bottle and put it in the freezer. After taking it out, observe the melting process, and pour some into a cup or stick your finger into it to feel how cold it is. If possible use a thermometer to take its temperature.

Let's play something

When playing a board game the child should count the dots on the dice a few times and they should move the figures on the board too.

Play with cards. It isn't necessary to play by the rules. The point is that the child looks for the similar cards and they can pick the ones that are different from the rest.

Opposites

Try to find the opposing concepts. Do this task in drawing.

Divide a sheet with a vertical line into two halves. You draw an image of a concept on your half and then the child draws an image of the opposite concept. Always name the concepts you draw.

For example:

thin man	fat man
small ball	big ball
tall tree	short tree
short pencil	long pencil
a lot of beads	few beads

February

 Who does the following jobs?
Here is a discussion game about occupations. Choose ones that are not completely new to the child. You can just talk about the rest of them.

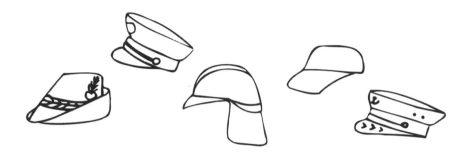

Who puts out the fire? (the fireman)
Who cures sick children? (the doctor)
Who looks after sick children in the hospital? (the nurse)
Who makes the bread we eat? (the baker)
Who produces wheat? (the farmer)
Who fixes bad teeth? (the dentist)
Who do you get salami from? (the shop assistant)
Who builds houses? (the builder)
Who keeps order in the streets? (the policeman/garda)
Who writes newspapers? (the journalist)
Who cures a sick cow? (the vet)
Who reads the news on TV? (the newsreader)
Who chops wood in the forest? (the woodcutter)
Who discovers new medicines? (the scientists)
Who fixes cars? (the mechanic)

(Divide these questions over two or three occasions.)

Play with their hands

Trace around the child's hand on a sheet. Name your fingers. Recite the following rhyme a couple of times.

'Tommy Thumb, Tommy Thumb, where are you?
Here I am, here I am, how do you do?
Peter Pointer, Peter Pointer, where are you?
Here I am, here I am, how do you do?
Toby Tall, Toby Tall, where are you?
Here I am, here I am, how do you do?
Ruby Ring, Ruby Ring, where are you?
Here I am, here I am, how do you do?
Baby Small, Baby Small, where are you?
Here I am, here I am, how do you do?
Fingers all, Fingers all, where are you?
Here we are, here we are, how do you do?'

Bring the finger drawings to life. Draw hair, eyes, ears, nose, mouth and clothes on them.

Another time turn your child's and your index fingers into human figures. Draw hair, eyes, ears, nose, mouth, a tie, etc. on the upper knuckle palm-side. Make a small skirt using a piece of cloth – now you are ready for the puppet show.

Place adverbs

'Be a robot.' Get a box and find something that fits into it. Ask your child to become a robot and follow instructions. You should change your voice into a 'robot voice'. (Robot language is broken, jerky talk.) 'Put the pen-cil in-to the box!' 'Put it in front of the box!' 'Put it be-hind the box!' 'Take the box to the front of the ward-robe, take the pen-cil out and put it in the draw-er!'

March

Geometric figures

Get to know the concepts of a circle, a triangle and a square.

Cut out shapes of various sizes using coloured paper: triangles, circles and squares.

Pick out 4-5 shapes at random and give them to your child to make a picture out of them. When it's finished, name the product and stick it on a blank sheet.

Later on, you can let your child pick out a few figures and arrange them whatever way they want to form a picture. Observe how much they get engaged in the activity.

Divide a sheet into two halves. You place a figure on one half and ask your child to place the same figure on their half so that you make a twin picture together. Name the geometric figures (circle, triangle and square) a good few times during this activity.

Cycle of life

People are born, they live and then they die.

Look at photographs or video images of your child from earlier times. Let them ask questions and tell them about their past.

Tell them about you being a child long ago and share a few interesting stories from your own childhood with them. Talk about them becoming a grown-up one day and that they will have children, whom they will love very much.

Mention that some old people get very tired and sometimes they get sick and eventually they die.

Plant a few seeds (beans or peas) in a small dish and observe how they develop into plants.

Observations outside

Go for outings, weather permitting.

Play ball and have a run around.

Observe what is occurring in nature, for example, the leaves are growing back on trees, new plants are growing.

Look for insects, snails and tadpoles. Pick moss and flowers.

Tell them the importance of respecting nature. Warn them not to destroy anything in nature with no good reason. They should not tear off leaves or be cruel to animals. Explain to them why this is important. Remind them that a flower picked is a seed lost.

Animals around the house

(Do these activities a few times during the month.)

Draw pictures of 3-4 animals, whatever ones the child wants and has seen (for example, a hen, a cat, a rabbit or a pig).

- Discuss which animal has feathers, a tail, hair, a beak, claws and hooves. Ask simple questions, such as: 'Which one has feathers? Which of them has a tail?'

- Tell your child about what these animals eat (for example, swill, feed, alfalfa, meat or seeds). To provide your child with new information simple questions can help, for example, 'Which animal eats swill? Which one eats feed?' Your child answers the question by pointing at a picture. (Discuss unknown concepts.)

- It is more difficult for the child if you expect them to answer the question with words, but you should try that as well anyway, for example, 'Where do hens, cats, rabbits or pigs live? What sort of sound do they make? What do we call the young ones, the mummy and the daddy animals?'

- On other occasions use the same aspects to talk about the following animals: cows, dogs, ducks, turkeys, horses, sheep, mice, goats, pigeons and geese.

How do little boys and little girls dress?

Look at magazines and discuss what clothes women wear and what clothes men wear. What will happen if you draw funny things in the pictures, such as a moustache, a beard, or a hat for a woman or a fancy necklace or long earrings with precious stones for a man?

Draw these funny things in magazine pictures and laugh together.

'Dress' animals, in magazines. You can have great fun by adding spectacles, a hat, a rucksack, or a pair of shoes to some pictures or putting a wristwatch on the cow's leg.

Your child should do most of the drawing.

Humming game

Hum a melody that's known to the child. Their task is to recognise it and sing it with the words. Do the inverse game, too. The child has to hum and you recognise the song.

May

Getting to know different vegetables
To learn about vegetables you could go out to your garden – if you have one. If you don't have a garden, you can look around at the market or look at pictures of vegetables in picture books or go to a garden centre or a farm.

The following vegetables should be part of the home curriculum: carrots, parsnips, cabbage, cauliflower, swede, onions, celery, lettuce, cucumber, tomatoes, peppers, peas and potatoes.

If possible, on one occasion put five of these vegetables on a plate and examine them one by one. The child should smell and have a taste of all of them.

Group them in a few different ways (for example, according to their colour or according to their shape).

Cut the vegetables in half and examine them again.

Memory game
Say the names of the vegetables on the plate aloud. After this the child should turn around and you should remove one vegetable off the plate. When the child turns back they have to guess which vegetable is missing. Let the child play with vegetables or help you to cook them. During these activities make the child practise their names. Allow them to slice vegetables with a plastic knife, so that they gather information about their hardness and their texture.

Human faces

Draw a few oval shapes to turn them into human faces. You and the child can add a nose, a mouth, eyes, hair and ears. Try to guess what mood these people are in. Give them a suitable name.

His/Her Highness says

Play kings and queens. The child is the king/queen and everything happens as they wish and order. They must be addressed as His/Her Highness, and people have to bow to them. They could have a crown, a sceptre and a cloak. You can use a plastic plant pot as the crown, a big wooden spoon as the sceptre and a large shawl as the cloak.

Entertain and sing to them and joke with them. However, you must take them seriously as royalty. Serve their food and drink on a tray. Pre-taste their food. Finally, end the festivities with a big dance.

You can invite a few other children to this reception.

June

 Get them acquainted with some fruits during the summer
Get them to taste the following fruits: apples, pears, plums, bananas, strawberries, raspberries, peaches, apricots, cherries, kiwis and melons. Discuss the following when having a taste of these fruits: (cut them in half before tasting them)
-The colour and taste of the fruit and the number of seeds
-What can you make out of it? (soup, sauce, jam or preserved fruit)
-Where does it grow? (on a tree, on a vine, on a bush or on the ground)

Play this guessing game: Which fruit is it?
'It is yellow, it is sour and we can put some of its juice in the lemonade.' (lemon)
Let the child give you a few riddles too.

 How many dots?
Draw three balls and ask the child to draw one dot on the first ball. Then ask them to draw one dot more on the second ball and one dot more on the third ball. Which ball has the most dots? Which ball has the least? Draw the following picture onto a sheet:

The child has to draw lines below the pictures of the balls to indicate how many dots each ball has.
Then do the reverse: draw a few balls with a different number of lines below each of them. The child has to draw dots on the ball to indicate how many lines there are below each ball.
(There shouldn't be more than three lines below a ball.)
Do this activity at least twice during the month.

 Play with jigsaw puzzles
Give the child a 10-16 piece jigsaw puzzle (if you don't have one at home, you could borrow one from a library or a friend). You should help your child put it together on the first few occasions. Do not put the puzzle together more than once on one occasion.

The summer

There is no programme to follow for the months of July and August. Families live more freely this time of the year, without routines, and often they go travelling or are on holidays.

However, if you are in the mood for a joint activity, you can take your pick of the activities over the past year.

In case you want to do your own hobby for a while or just to have a rest, you can offer your child an idea for some independent play.

Ideas for independent play

Give your child a magazine, a pair of safety scissors, a sheet of paper or cardboard and some glue. They will find out themselves what to do with them.

Place a building kit, a few toy cars and a few small dolls in the middle of the room without saying a word.

Leave some play dough, a few buttons and a selection of spices (peppercorns, cloves, mustard seeds, or cumin seeds) on the table.

Offer a topic for making a drawing: a lake with fish in it, a busy road or the big mushroom under which animals live, etc.

The child can pick flowers.

They can make a necklace using a number of good size beads.

They can build a sandcastle.

They can make a hut for themselves out of blankets.

They can do some target throwing.

They can help with the housework: to do some dusting, to wipe the tiles with a wet cloth, to brush the floor, to wash their socks, etc.

They can play ball, go on their bicycle or play with Lego.

They could make a flower arrangement for the kitchen table out of dry or cut flowers. The flowers can be pushed into some play dough.

Allow them to invite friends over and play with them.

However, do not let them get bored, watch TV all the time or play meaningless games.

Family games

Naturally, children demand joint play even during the summer. It is good to have a bit of brain training and fun these days as well. Here are a few ideas for times like that:

Which animal am I?

Imitate the noises they make or describe their looks and their lifestyle.

What's mummy/daddy/Peter doing?

Ask the question: 'What's daddy doing?' and show an action using mime. The child has to guess. Later, the child can do the actions.

A few ideas: shaving, brushing their teeth, reading the paper, tying their shoelaces, eating, driving the car, fixing something, washing the dishes, watching TV, stroking a dog, building, etc.

Situational games

These games are excellent for developing communication skills.

(During the game teach your child ways of greeting and addressing people, and a few rules of courtesy.)

Some situations: shopping – in a vegetable shop, or in a clothes shop; how to behave in a doctor's waiting room, when visiting friends (offering and asking for things); when travelling – asking about somebody's name, destination, or family.

Let the child act out conflict situations as well, and give them help to resolve the conflicts.

Play hide and seek

Play chasing starting with 'Eeny meeny' or some other rhyme to pick out the person who will chase after the other, after agreeing on the rules.

Continue my story

Start telling any friendly story and after a while pass it on to the child. The child then passes it back to you, and so on.

Pick the odd one out

Before starting the game tell the child about the cuckoo bird. Tell them that this bird lays her eggs into a different type of bird's nest, next to that bird's eggs, and her eggs don't belong in the nest.

'Pick the word that doesn't belong to the other words.' For example, hat, shoe, roast chicken – the third one is a dish, while the other two are articles of clothing.

Fruit cake, light bulb, melon – the second one is an object, not food.

Horse, donkey, watering can – the third one is not an animal.

Pickaxe, pencil, pen – the first one is not for writing with.

Ladybird, snail, butterfly – the second one cannot fly.

If the child is very smart make it harder for them by giving them more difficult exercises.

If the child gives an answer that is different from what you had in mind and they have a logical explanation you should by all means accept the answer. Give them praise and tell them your answer, too.

You can also use pictures for this activity.

'Cross the odd one out.'

Description of the child
at the end of the 4th year

Height: cm/inch

Weight: kg/lbs

Movements:

Some of their features:

Typical activities:

Level of speech development:

Favourite toys:

Favourite food:

Favourite books:

Some of their friends:

Developmental activities
for children aged 4-5 years

In September, after the summer holiday, life gets back to normal, to the usual working days. Over the summer your child will develop and progress both physically and mentally. Continue to support them and to provide them with a greater knowledge of the world – just like you did during the previous years.

The mental capacity of a 4-5 year old child is surprisingly large. They are getting a huge amount of information from their peers and from the television, too. However, this knowledge is very unstable. There are a lot of uncertainties and misunderstandings in it. The reason for this is that reality and fantasy get mixed up in the child's mind. Joint play, practice and learning together will strengthen their knowledge and correct any mistakes. Parents do not have to try and help their children to understand all the connections of cause and effect between things. This will develop later anyway. Parent-child activities offer children the chance to ask questions and parents to provide the right information. That's why it is so important that parent and child listen only to each other during each session. These occasions supply the child with a huge amount of extra knowledge mentally, but children also benefit a great deal from it emotionally.

In this chapter you will find monthly programmes, like in the previous one, but I have increased the number of activities for each month believing that this will match the child's improved efficiency. During this chapter the following areas will be covered: mathematics, environmental studies, language skills, dexterity, motor skills, thinking and memory skills, rules of courtesy, safety advice and independent play.

Every month there is an additional task to practise and a courtesy rule, which will ensure that your child leaves a good impression wherever they go. Discuss the importance of keeping these rules and create situations where they can practise them.

The number of activities that require thinking and concentration skills also increases at this level.

The way to do the activities is to do 1 or 2 activities weekly on 1 or 2 occasions. Repeat the same activity at least once more during the same month. If an activity or topic causes difficulties to your child, mark it with a red dot and do it again at a later time, even after a few months.

Have a good time and have fun when doing the tasks.

September

Courtesy rule: Greet people

People form an opinion of us by looking at our behaviour and listening to what we say and how we say it. It is important that children learn to be courteous and observe other people being courteous and respectful. Greeting and addressing people is an important part of human communication. We must greet people we know the proper way. The child should address grown-ups with respect, for example, 'Excuse me, Miss'; 'Please, Mr Taylor!'

Build in saying hello and addressing people in situational games.

Let's learn about traffic

The main task of the month for September should be to practise how to be out and about in an appropriate way.

Teach the child how to look around before crossing the road. Practise this together when you are walking to school, going shopping, etc. Tell the child that they need to move fast when crossing the road but they mustn't run.

Teach them to be careful but make sure they do not develop a fear of traffic.

Let them show you the way home after some walks. If possible, try to go various directions so that they get to know all paths that lead to your home well. Help them by giving clues, for example, 'Can you see the newspaper stand? This is where you have to cross to the other side.'

In big cities, where traffic lights direct traffic, it is highly important that children look at the traffic lights. It is wrong to teach that the child should start crossing when they see grown-ups doing it. A lot of grown-ups are careless and they break the lights, if they think it is safe to do so.

The child already knows the colours of the lights so it only takes a little bit of practice to learn the rules.

Sing a song:
'The Animals Went in Two by Two...'

How do animals move?

Here's a good game to play at this age. This game enhances mimicking skills, imagination and bodily awareness.

If the animal that you mention to the child flies, the child should imitate flying; if it jumps, the child should jump; and if the animal crawls, the child should crawl on all fours. (The game can be played without movements, only in words.)

You should ask the title question and the child can respond with a movement or a word.

Butterflies fly.
Ducks waddle.
Rabbits hop.
Storks walk and fly.
Frogs jump.
Snails slither.
Ladybirds crawl and fly.
Dogs walk and run.
Ants crawl.
Fish swim.
Swallows fly.
Tigers walk and run.
Grasshoppers jump and fly.
Mice run.
Flies fly.
Woodpeckers fly.
Sparrows hop and fly.
Snakes slither and swim.
Lizards crawl.
Pigs walk and run.

Let's examine our faces

Sit next to your child in front of a mirror. Examine both of your faces. Look for the eyebrows and the eyelashes. Find out what colour your eyes are. Examine both of your noses.

Examine your tongues and then move on to looking at your teeth. Tap your teeth gently to see how hard and strong they are. Eat a piece of fruit in front of the mirror. Point out that we use our front teeth to bite pieces off food and that we use the back teeth for grinding. Look and see if any fruit has stayed on your teeth after swallowing the last piece.

Teach your child how to brush their teeth properly. Practise in front of the mirror, and show your child how to give teeth a thorough clean. Do this a good few times.

October

Courtesy rule: Wash your hands

We always wash our hands before eating. The main reason for this is that germs must be removed from our hands so that we avoid eating them with the food and getting sick.

Let the child lay the table and help themselves to the food at family dinners. Encourage them to pass items on the table and offer food to the other people at the table, for example, a basket/plate of bread.

Practise eating with a knife and a fork and using a spoon.

Finding our way on a map

Draw a map onto a big piece of cardboard. Make the roads wide enough to push some toy cars along them. Draw the main buildings of your area onto the map. You can also draw a few bushes and trees. Put a grocery shop, a school, a doctor's surgery, etc. on your map. Play together on the finished map. Lego people are an ideal size for moving around on your map.

How many buttons can I count?

Use a bag of buttons in various colours for this activity. Ask the child to make colour groups. Give them the same number of cups or little bowls as the number of the colour groups.

- There should be 3 buttons of the same colour in every cup.

Ask your child to divide the 3 buttons between you fairly. They will soon realise that it is impossible. You could say: 'Yes, because three is an uneven or odd number.'

Try the same task with four and five buttons. Make a note of which numbers are even and which ones are odd numbers.

- Make a pattern using three different colours (for example, red-yellow-blue, red-yellow-blue) and ask your child to continue the pattern the same way.

Use a few small pieces of square shaped paper and put the dot image of the numbers on these paper squares using buttons.

Then ask your child which square has 2, 4, 1, 5 and 3 buttons on it. (It is okay if the child makes mistakes, as they are only starting to learn the numbers.)

Enjoy the game.

Let's illustrate a poem
Look for a poem that has characters in it that are easy to draw a picture of before the game. Read out the poem slowly, paying attention to the tone of your voice. Then ask your child to draw a picture of something that comes to mind after hearing the poem. Let them talk about the poem or the topic while doing the drawing. Ask them if they liked it and whether it was a happy poem or a sad one.

Guess who it is
Teach your child how to solve riddles. Ask them to make up similar ones and you should try to find out the concepts by using the description your child gives you.
Start with simple ones so that they get to like them.
Which animal am I thinking of?
'It is hairy, it likes meat and some of them bite you.' (dog, wolf)
'It lives in water, it has scales and it's a good swimmer.' (fish)
'It loves carrots.' (rabbit)
'It grazes on leaves high up with its long neck.' (giraffe)

Sing a song:
'Pussycat, Pussycat, where have you been?'
Clap along.

November

Courtesy rule: Use a tissue
Every time we sneeze or cough we cover our mouth and nose with our hand, or even better we sneeze and cough into a tissue. Do not let them pick their nose as it can develop into a nasty habit. Explain that they can use a tissue and blow their nose.
Watch whether they bite their nails. If they do, try and encourage them to stop it.

Learn the secondary colours
By this time your child will know the primary colours (red, yellow and blue) and it will be a real challenge for them to experience how new colours (secondary colours: purple, green and orange) can be produced by mixing the primary colours together, two at a time. Copy this drawing onto a sheet.

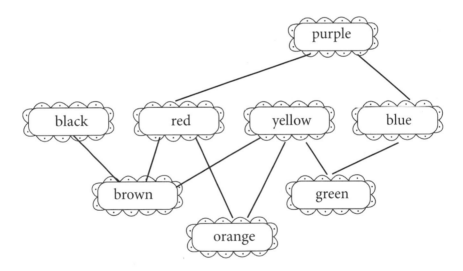

Draw a dot in the four middle oval shapes with the appropriate colours with coloured pencils. The child should paint each oval shape the same colour as the dot inside.
Then ask the child to mix the colours following the diagram and use the colour they get to paint the other four oval shapes above and below the four original shapes. (For example, blue + red = purple)
If the child is still happy to do more painting, you can draw a picture of a boy and a girl onto a bigger sheet and let your child paint their clothes using the various colours they mixed.

Play shopkeeper
Use real money to buy real toys in your shop.
The point of this game is that the child gets to count their money as much as possible.
They should not keep the money in their hands but put it on the table and, as much as possible, arrange the coins according to the dot images you used in the previous month.
You should make the child buy more of the '1-coin' toys and get them to count how much they have to pay. (Do not confuse them by giving them difficult calculations.)

Who is the story teller today?
Ask the child a couple of times during the month to tell you their favourite story. It could be a story they hear in playschool, their childminder's or one of their favourite books from home or the library.

Practise marching to the beat of some songs.

What do they like to eat?
Ask this question about the following animals and let the child answer:
Horses – oats, hay, grass
Pigs – swill, apples, carrots
Birds – caterpillars
Dogs – meat
Rabbits – carrots, cabbage
Hens – seeds
Foxes – rabbits, hens
Frogs – mosquitoes, flies
Swallows – flies, other insects
Ladybirds – green flies

December

Enjoy the magic and excitement of this month with your child. Show them how to get ready for Christmas and prepare them for the great celebration.

Similarly to last year, tell your child about the origins of Christmas and some folk traditions.

Prepare for it actively. Give them simple tasks, for example, 'Will you bring me two eggs, please?', 'Stir this cream for a while', 'Can you clear the table for me?'

Listen to Christmas and seasonal songs a number of times during the month. Arouse their interest in the celebrations. It is natural that for a child presents are the most important part of Christmas. However, the warm atmosphere around the house will remain in their memory for a long time, even throughout their adulthood when they will have happy memories of these past Christmases.

Eating your dinner by candlelight, peaceful and calm singing, praying and listening to music together will help enrich their emotional wellbeing.

The presents the child gets for Christmas hold a real value to them if you play with them together.

My advice is the same as before: during the holidays try to spend as much time with your child as possible playing or going out together. Christmas is also about family time. This might be a good time to bring them to other relatives' homes and explain the family connection, for example, cousins, aunts, uncles, etc.

How to tie a bow and how to plait

Boys should also learn these things.

Making a bow can be practised by using a wide ribbon tied onto a chair or table leg. Follow the steps below.

1. Show your child how to cross the two strands and how to stretch them on something by pulling.

2. Help them form a 'rabbit's ear', a loop, and put the other strand over it. Give the child a hand with pulling it out through the right hole.

3. Stretch the bow and arrange the loops nicely.

The child should always say what they were actually doing.

If your child cannot do any of the steps do not force them to try harder. You can just leave the task for the time being and try it again after 1 or 2 months.

Start teaching how to plait with a demonstration, by using two play dough worms. If the child is able to work with two strands move on to three strands. The best thing is to have three dough worms, a different colour each. The only thing to explain to your child is that they should only move the sole strand to the other side and place it between the other two strands. Then they should look at the other side and find the new sole strand and move it across and place it between the two strands that are together.

On another occasion you can use thick wool to make some plaits.

Reply with something
The task is to do association of ideas. After you say a word the child is asked to say another word that comes to their mind. They can say an adjective, another noun or an action word also. It's a great mind exercise. However, do not try to make the child participate if they are tired – this would not be fun.

> For example, Christmas – presents
> Toy car – fast, red
> Candle – light
> Snow – white, cold
> Sweetbread – tasty

Naturally, you can choose words in other areas, for example, dog, fish, TV, pipe, cup, etc.

Listen to Christmas songs
> For example, 'Jingle Bells'
> 'Christmas is Coming'
> 'Silent Night'
> 'Hark the Herald Angels Sing'
> 'Away in a Manger'
> 'The Twelve Days of Christmas'
> 'We Wish You a Merry Christmas'

January

Courtesy Rule: Blow your nose properly
We blow our nose into a tissue or handkerchief. Show the child how to blow one nostril at a time, while blocking the other one, and then do the opposite. Tell your child to throw the used tissues into the bin.

Let's create patterns
Fold a sheet into four parts vertically, like an accordion. Rotate the page and draw simple shapes at the beginning of the lines, 'for example':

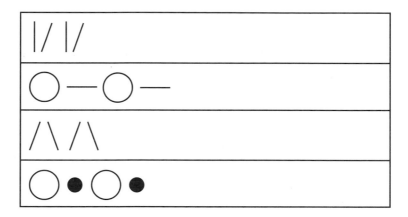

If your child likes this task they can make up patterns themselves.

Fold paper napkins
Fold a napkin diagonally twice, then open it. Fold up one side so that you get a small container. You can stick it onto the side of a wardrobe and keep small things in it. You can also decorate it by drawing on it or gluing things on it.

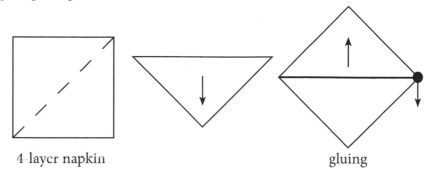

4 layer napkin   gluing

Fold a napkin to make a fan. If you tie a bright ribbon around the centre you can make a nice butterfly out of it. After making a few butterflies you can hang them up on the living room light – it will be a nice decoration.

Tie the ribbon around here

When you are doing some folding, the child should sit next to you. After doing a fold wait for your child until they do the same. You should not help them, unless you feel that the task is too difficult for them. Let your child keep trying.

 I'll steal your story
Choose a story that both of you know well. You can start telling the story, but you have to stop if the child puts their hand over your mouth. After this they can continue the story until you steal the right of story telling back from them, etc. Let the child speak longer but when you are telling the story you might want to pretend that you don't want to stop by holding their hand.
Have fun stealing the story; play this game often.

 Looking for opposites

You say:	Your child says:
If I'm soft	I'm hard
Loose	tight
Light	heavy
Silly	smart
Bad	good
Cold	hot
Ugly	beautiful
Tall	short
Black	white
Big	small

What do you call…?

Try the following game. If your child doesn't understand do not lose heart, and get back to it some time later.

The task is to find a first name that starts with the same letter as the first letter of the occupation.

What do you call		
	the engine driver?	Erika
	the ticket inspector?	Terence
	the policeman?	Paul
	the pilot?	Penelope
	the soldier?	Sam

Listen to children's songs on a CD

Pick one of the songs and learn the words by heart. Sing it without the music as well.

Courtesy rule: Say thank you

Draw your child's attention to saying thank you kindly for any help, food or other favours they get. Do this often.

During the month check if your child is making progress in this area. It is not enough to simply tell them to say thank you or to ask them 'Did you say thank you?' You should analyse a few situations. Focus their attention on the fact that people respond to others doing them favours by saying kind words or by giving back a smile – and that this is the nice way of doing things.

Dressing up

Make playtime at home happy by giving the child old clothes, shoes and hats and imagining you are someone else. Drink some (herbal) tea, eat some snacks and pretend you are real princesses and heroes.

Selecting buttons

You will need: 10 small white, 5 small black, 5 big black, 5 red and 5 big white buttons.

Arrange the buttons according to a certain rule.

The child should continue the following logical patterns:

2 small white – 1 small black –

1 small white – 1 small black – 1 red –1 big white – 1 small black –

(they need to start paying attention to both size and colour from now on)

2 big black – 1 small black –

2 big black – 1 small white –

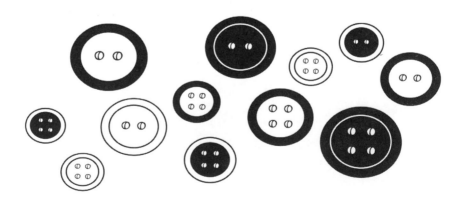

Looking for objects

Look for objects that you use for keeping things in from around the house. Gather them onto a blanket, cover them with a cloth and take turns picking one out. You and your child should name the object and the thing(s) you keep in it. Then whoever picked the object should find its original place in the house and put it back. Both of you should make sure that the other person finds the right place for each object. You can pretend that you're trying to trick your child. Some examples for objects to use in this game: a cereal box, a phone book, toothpaste, a saucepan, a vase, a pencil case, beauty product (e.g. face cream) tubs, a DVD case, a glasses case, etc.

Winter sports

Have a chat about winter sports.

On a few occasions look for TV programmes where the child can see people doing winter sports. Talk about the programmes and let the child ask questions. Try the Eurosport channel – they often broadcast the programmes you need.

You can mention skating, skiing, ski-jumping, ice hockey and cross-country skiing.

The two of us have two hands

This is a really fun game. By playing this game you can improve the skill of focusing on each other and the child's adaptation skills. Tidy a shelf, but beforehand tie together your right arm and your child's left arm, and your right leg and your child's left leg using pieces of ribbon. (If your child is left-handed, then do it the other way round, so that their left hand is free.)

You are not allowed to use those hands that are tied together, you can only use your free hands. Of course, the tied up legs will make your job more difficult.

Carry out other easy tasks also like this (for example, make your beds, wash your faces, brush your teeth, fold your clothes, or brush the floor).

Courtesy rule: Do not push
Draw your child's attention to being courteous and not pushing their way forward.
Ask them to practise with you. They should let you go out through the door first or if they go out first they should hold the door for you. Do not expect your child to behave like this just yet when you are using public transport.

Look at pictures of birds in books
Look for pictures of the most common birds: pigeons, sparrows, owls, herons, cuckoos, magpies, robins and swallows (it is unnecessary to teach the exact names of each species at this level).
Talk about the birds 2 or 3 times during the month. Examine three birds at a time. Pick ones that the child has already seen, if you can (for example, 1. swallow – owl – heron, 2. sparrow – tit – starling).
Guidelines:
- 'Show me how big each of the birds is in reality.'
- 'Which one is the biggest, and which is the smallest?'
- 'What does each of the birds eat?'
(Swallows eat insects, owls eat mice and other rodents, sparrows eat seeds, tits eat seeds and insects, etc.)
Parallel to this last question, discuss which birds are useful and which are harmful. Talk about the magpie being a thief and the cuckoo who makes other birds bring up their chicks.

Let's play cards
Play with a pack of children's play cards. If your child already knows how to find matching pairs tell them about the rules. It is fine to play with the cards facing up at first. This way you can help the child make decisions and they can learn from your decisions, too. When your child gets the idea of the game, you can turn the cards face down.
Take the cards out a good few times during the month. It can be fun to see your child
wanting to win and see them getting excited about winning. After lots of turns, your child will slowly have to learn about losing as well.

How do machines work?

Do not think big when you are reading this question.

Show your child how the hoover or a coffee grinder works. Take them apart if you can and talk about the function of each part. Let them try to work the machines but draw their attention to the potential danger. Stress that they are only allowed to play with the machines if a responsible grown-up is supervising them.

Find out how bicycles work.

Turn a bicycle upside down and let your child move the pedal by hand to see how the wheel is turning.

Show them how to turn on and off the television, the radio, the tape-, CD- or MP3 player and the video or DVD-player.

However, they shouldn't be allowed to turn these appliances on or off for no reason. If the child does this, you should forbid them to touch the machines and explain to them the danger of breaking them or getting hurt. Also, this is a good time to explain the importance of turning machines off to conserve energy.

Riddles

I'm running without legs
I'm your friend but your worst enemy
I'm clear but you can see me
What am I?   (Water)

What is found over your head but under your hat?
(Your hair)

I am purple, yellow, red and green
The King cannot reach me and neither can the Queen.
I show my colours after the rain
And only when the sun comes out again.
(A rainbow)

Look at my face and you see somebody
Look at my back and you see nobody.
(A mirror)

First, you will see me in the grass, bright as a yellow sun
Then I change to dainty white and blow away…
alas, my time is done. (A dandelion)

I love your dog and ride on his back
I travel for miles but don't leave a track. (A flea)

I have a mouth but cannot eat. (A river)

I have a face but cannot see. (A clock)

We have legs but cannot walk. (Tables/chairs)
What always goes to sleep with his shoes on? (A horse)

What do you call an old snowman? (Water)

What is there in an empty jug? (Air)

It has two ears but it cannot hear. (A pot)

Which is the strongest animal in the world? (The snail, because it carries its house on its back.)

I'm white when you throw me up in the air, but I'm yellow after falling down. What am I? (An egg)

It can spin but it's not a weaver. What is it? (A spider)

It's a white blanket, it's not made down here but it comes from the sky. (Snow)

It has no guitar or harp, but it still makes music. What is it? (A cricket)

April

Courtesy rule: Do not litter
Teach your child how to use the litterbins. Do not let them touch them or lean into them. Ask them to put the rubbish into the bins when you are at home, too.

Continue the pattern
Fold a sheet into three parts like an accordion. Make patterns in writing. You can help your child when they are doing the second or third line if they ask you to do so. If the child gets tired fast it is enough if they circle around the shapes with the appropriate colours.
B - blue, R - red, Y - yellow

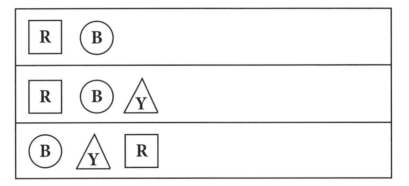

Animals who live near us
What animals live in the wild in our country? Why are there zoos?
Talk about animals while looking at picture books: the deer, the squirrel, the hedgehog, the seal and the badger.
Talk about:
-where these animals live and
-what they eat.
The deer is herbivorous and eats grass and undergrowth, the badger is omnivorous and eats plants as well as insects, the seal is carnivorous and eats fish, and the squirrel is a rodent and eats plants, nuts and seeds.
Animals from far away lands and animals who hide, and therefore they are difficult to see in our country, live in zoos.
When you talk about animals in the zoo, mention only if they live in a warm or a cold country and what they like to eat. No further details are necessary at this stage.

Let's play theatre!
Ask your child's friends or cousins to come over to your house. Tell them that you are going to put on a show. Ask them to either sing a song, say a poem, do a dance or do something funny.
Turn the sofa/couch or the bed into a stage for their performances. The audience can sit on the floor in front of them. When the show is over and everyone has applauded, you can have a little party. You can play party games, do some dancing and have some snacks.

 Clap it back
Clap a rhythm of your choice to your child. They will have to clap what they heard back to you.
Sing some songs and clap along.
Hum a melody to your child who will have to copy you humming the same melody.

May

Courtesy rule: Be tidy
Draw your child's attention to keeping their surroundings tidy. Tell them that toys and clothes have a regular place where they are put back when they are not in use. Practise folding some clothes together. You could encourage them to make their bed every morning, with a little help from you at first.

Let's go on an outing!
Go on shorter or longer outings a few times during the summer. Look for wild flowers. Name a few flowers, whichever you know the name of yourself.

The most common ones: dandelion, daisy, violet, forget-me-not, bluebell, chamomile, daffodil, shamrock, primrose, buttercup and foxglove. (You can make a wreath out of dandelions and a necklace out of daisies.)

Take a few flowers apart. Find their stamens and their pistil.

Tell your child that bees visit flowers to get the pollen. Point out trees that you know the name of to your child whenever you are walking in the woods. The most common ones are the oak, the beech, the pine, the chestnut, the sycamore and the ash.

Go up to the trees and see if you can stretch your arms around the trunk. Discuss the different trees. Examine their leaves, the colour of their trunks, their shape and their size. Search for some insects, for example, snails, worms, flies, beetles or woodlice. Stress the importance of respecting nature and being kind to animals and insects.

Play with finger puppets

Draw faces on your index fingers. Name these characters.

Act out a short scene. Let your child pick the topic, but you can help them by giving them a few ideas. (For example, meeting a friend, talking about playschool, brothers and sisters, grandparents, children's TV-programmes, shopping or travelling.)

You can pick out one of the child's drawings together and use it as the backdrop for your little play.

If you cut small holes in a sheet of paper they can be windows of a house and your characters can be the people who live in the house.

Play with play dough together

Choose any topic you like.

If you don't have any ideas, make a basket or a nest by braiding three strands of dough.

Roll some eggs and put them in the nest or the basket.

Make simple animal figures, such as ducks (a big one and a few small ones), a snail, a snake and a rabbit.

Bring the dough figures to life and pretend they are chatting.

You can also make reeds, a fence or something else by using matchsticks.

Should it fly or not?

After a short rhyme of your choice say: 'Here flies, here flies the ...' The child will have to raise their arms if they hear a name of an object or a living thing that really can fly.

Let the child be the 'driver'.

'Here flies, here flies the ... boat, parrot, chair, flower, aeroplane, rabbit, sparrow, swallow, spoon, helicopter, etc.'

June

Courtesy rule: No splashing
You have to pay attention to others when swimming. It is bad manners to splash other people or to throw a ball at them. If it happens you have to apologise. The child can say: 'I'm sorry for splashing you.'

Play tourists
Go for a walk near where you live and pretend that your child is a tourist and you are the tour guide. Visit the most important buildings in your area, such as the town hall, the doctor's surgery, the local store, the post office, the pharmacy and the library. Have a look at any statues or churches you may bump into on your tour. Draw your child's attention to any architectural beauties, any decorative facades, any stained glass windows, etc.

On one or two occasions swap roles so you can be the tourist and the child can play the role of the guide.

As a follow-up to their experience as a tourist, let your child paint on a glass window or tiles with tempera paint. Or they can paint on a jar, a mirror, a piece of wood or some textile. Show the child that they are only allowed to paint the areas you marked. The colours you use should be the most important part of this project.

Dominoes

Teach your child how to play with dominoes. You can initially use dominoes with figures on them, but a child who can play cards will be able to recognise the identical dominoes that have dots on them quickly. There is no need to keep asking the child how many dots they can see on a particular domino. But sometimes, especially when there are five or fewer dots on a domino, you can ask: 'Let's see, what number do I have to put down now?' This way the dot image will become firmly rooted in the child's memory.

What vegetables or fruit do we need for these dishes?

Your child will be the chef and you will be the chef's assistant who goes to the market to buy the fruit and vegetables that are needed for the cooking.

You read out the menu and your child makes a list of the fruit and vegetables they will need.

On the menu you can have the following dishes:

Bacon and cabbage – cabbage
Fish and chips – potatoes
Mushroom soup – mushrooms, onions
Garlic bread – garlic
Blueberry muffin – blueberries
Tomato salad – tomatoes
Roast chicken – none
Carrot cake – carrots
BLT sandwich – lettuce, tomatoes
Seafood chowder – potatoes, carrots, leeks
Cheese tortellini – none
Baked beans – tomatoes
Stew – potatoes, carrots, onions

July

Courtesy rule: Wait nicely
Talk about the rules of standing in a queue.
Tell your child not to push themselves forward but wait patiently until it's their turn. Let your child do some shopping on their own with you close to them, but let them hand over the item, give the money and wait for the change and the receipt. Explain to them what a receipt is and that it is important to hold onto it in case you need to return the item you bought.

What is made of wheat?
Whenever you travel around the country show your child wheat fields and stress how important this plant is. Take some seeds out of the ear and grind them between two stones. You will end up with some coarse wheat meal. If you continued grinding it you would get flour.
(Talk about hulling as well.)
You can make a number of pastas or other food by mixing flour, water, and eggs or yeast together. Knead some dough and make various shapes and figures out of it. Bake them.
Try to collect lots of different foods that are made of flour, for example, bread, bread buns, rolls, scones, pancakes and dry pastas.
Go to a bakery, look at the selection and name each product.
If you don't want to bother with making real dough, then you can mix 1 part flour, 1 part salt and some water together to make salt and flour dough. The child can use this for making shapes such as plaited bread, rolls.
During the summer, whenever you are doing some baking involve your child as well.

Hearing or seeing?

The child doesn't say a word during this game. If they hear the name of an object that can be seen (rather than heard) they should point to their eyes, and if they hear the name of an object that can be heard (rather than seen) they should push their ear slightly forward, as if they were listening to something. First, you should show the child how to use these gestures.

aeroplane – hearing	telephone – hearing
rainbow – seeing	whistle – hearing
horse neighing – hearing	computer – seeing
telescope – seeing	guitar – hearing
radio – hearing	birds singing – hearing
television – seeing	a bunch of flowers – seeing
bell ringing – hearing	picture book – seeing
magnifying glass – seeing	earphones – hearing

Let's eat some ice cream!

Draw an ice cream cone on a sheet of paper. Ask your child to draw another four cones. How many children can have ice cream?

Pretend that you buy everybody an ice cream cone. Draw in the ice cream scoops on the cones. Plan in advance how many scoops each of the children can eat and colour in the scoops according to the type of ice cream. (There shouldn't be more than five scoops.) For example:

Sean	Anna
chocolate	strawberry
vanilla	lemon
strawberry	blueberry
	pineapple

Sand play

If you don't have a sand pit, you could bring your child to the beach or to a park/playground with a sand pit. Your child can draw or pick some flowers or leaves to decorate 'cakes' with them. They can prepare little flags using a stick and paper to put them on the top of the sandcastles. If there are more children playing together they can try and take the castle from each other. There should be two groups. When the castle is built the members of the two groups should stand on opposite sides of the castle with opposite flags in their hands. They can use sand bombs to shoot at the castle. Whoever hits the castle within a marked area can put on their flag at the place of the impact. The winner is the team who have more of their flags on the castle, for example, out of ten attacks. (An adult should co-ordinate this game.)

August

Courtesy rule: Be independent

Set up a routine that can be followed from September onwards.

The child should have their own jobs, such as: going to the toilet independently, washing, having breakfast, brushing their teeth, getting dressed and making their bed.

Be an architect

Draw the front view of a castle taking into consideration the selection of building blocks you have. This castle should consist of at least 20-25 blocks. To carry out the task of building the castle following the plan requires concentrated attention, so reward your child if they are successful in this.

You can prepare the plan by building the castle yourself first, then drawing the front view followed by knocking down the structure. The child can then re-build it. If the task turns out to be too easy, you can draw the two side views of the castle as well, so that your child will have to build the right and left wings, too.

Do not mark colours by writing the first letters in but use real colouring instead, or else use a coloured strip that marks the colour of each block.

What belongs to the object?
The child's task in this game is to name a part of the object you call out. You should give a few examples first so that the child understands what to do.

> For example: clock – arm
> radio – button
> pen – tip, top
> slippers – bow, sole
> book – letter
> table – leg, tablecloth
> door – door handle, key
> ear – earring
> umbrella – handle
> pot – flower, earth
> toothbrush – bristles, toothpaste
> stairs – railing
> bicycle – pedal
> police car – siren
> television – remote control, screen
> basket – handle

Let's party!
Listen to songs that you both know on a tape or a CD. Dance and sing along.

Finish my drawing
The child has to use their imagination and turn a simple shape you drew into something else by adding to it in drawing. Show your child a few examples, as this task is not as simple as it sounds.

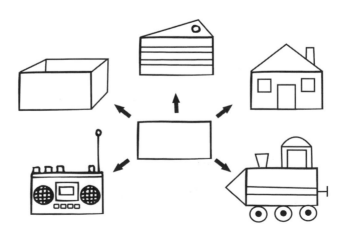

Description of the child
at the end of the 5th year

Height: cm/inch

Weight: kg/lbs

Movements:

Some of their features:

Typical activities:

Level of speech development:

Favourite toys:

Favourite food:

Favourite books:

Some of their friends:

Developmental activities
for children aged 5-6 years

Children between the ages of 5-6 years are extremely open to learning all kinds of new things. They are interested in almost everything and they are able to understand most of the simple connections between phenomena. They can draw conclusions from their own experiences, which may very often make grown-ups smile.

They are tremendously drawn to the world of tales and stories, and they tend to identify themselves with the hero. Children of this age love everything that requires them to use their imagination – because of this, they like playing together and distribute the various roles among themselves. They are happy about their freshly learnt skills, and they are becoming more and more ready for acquiring more serious knowledge as well. These children are fond of manual activities, which promote the development of their dexterity.

Taking into consideration these age specific features, parents can motivate their young children in many different ways so that the child's personality unfolds, which makes their strengths become obvious and provides a basis to build on. This process also makes their weaknesses stand out, so these can be dealt with by the parents focusing on them more. Spending time with the child enables the parents to get to know their child, as well as giving an opportunity for the child to find out how their parents think.

Try to spend even more time than before on doing things with your child. Take every opportunity to carry out the tasks. Use moments of walking home, drying the child after their bath and also the Sunday afternoon free time to play educational games with your child.

Of course, it is not a good idea to impose tasks on the child when they are tired.

Tasks should not be done out of responsibility, but for fun. You should always try to match the games with your own and your child's mood.

In the month-by-month programme there is a courtesy rule or safety advice, and there are different tasks, which offer you a wide range of activities. You should do at least two sessions per week, learning together with your child on two different days.

Read through the monthly programme and put it in your diary deciding what would be the best time for doing the sessions. If possible, pick the same days week by week so the child can develop a sense of regularity. Tasks that turn out to be too difficult should be marked and you can do them again at a later time.

If the child refuses to co-operate, do not accept it every time they do it. They need to get used to focusing their attention and get used to the idea that these activities are part of the weekly schedule. Part of the aim of this book is to increase the child's success rate at learning and to help them gradually gain self-confidence.

Have a ball and enjoy your work.

Safety advice: Do not play with the stove/oven/cooker
Teach your child how to light the gas fire or how to turn on the electric hob on the cooker under your supervision. Explain to them about the dangers of gas leakage. Discuss everything important in relation to handling hot objects and hot food. Most parents may have serious issues with this activity for children of this age but this way they can prevent their children from trying – out of curiosity – dangerous things on their own, without proper supervision.

 Which group has more? (Estimates)
To carry out this task you will need some small objects, such as buttons, coins or plastic discs. Take at least twenty of them.
• Make two groups at random, and ask the child to guess which group has more objects in it. Count them to see if the child was right.
• Ask them to make three identical groups. Count the objects in each group and distribute them between the three groups evenly. The best way to do this is to arrange the objects according to the dot image (images on a dice) of the appropriate number of the objects.
• Arrange six coins in a row. The child is then asked to add one more coin and to count how many coins they have.

• Arrange the coins like a domino.

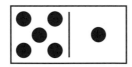 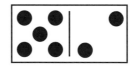

• Arrange fewer than five objects like different numbers on the domino.

The food journey
Ask your child to tell you where food goes after eating it.
For example: 'You chew the bread with your teeth, your tongue then mixes it with saliva so it turns into pulp. This pulp can slide down more easily through a long tube that's called the food pipe.'
Place your child's hand on their larynx so they can feel the movement every time they swallow. Next, place their hand below their ribs and name the stomach. Say: 'If you eat too much or you don't like the food you eat, your stomach may hurt. Inside your tummy the good food gets digested and absorbed into your body. The waste you don't need goes into tubes called your intestines.'
'Your intestines are long, coiled up tubes; the bread gets pulpier and pulpier in them. Whatever your body doesn't need because it cannot be digested you will get rid of in the form of poo.' (Further discussion of the topic is unnecessary.)
Try to mark the way of the food using a red pencil.

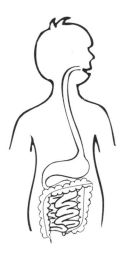

Memory game
Put three objects (for example, a pen, an eraser and a button) on the table in front of the child. Cover them with a cloth. Ask the child to leave the room or look away and change the position of the objects. When they come back they have to tell the difference.
If the child can tell the difference between the positions of three objects you can play with four or even five objects – but this is really hard. If the child can remember this, give them praise – tell them how great they are.

You are a real painter
Take some pencils and a sketch book with you for your
walk. Imagine that the animals you meet on your way
want to have a portrait made of them.
Look for a snail, a ladybird, a butterfly, an earthworm, etc.
Put each of them on a white sheet and try to draw a picture
of them. You can talk to the model (insect) during the preparation for
the drawing. You can play the role of the models and talk on their behalf.
You can add funny details to your drawings – they can be educational
elements, for example, the snail can get glasses, as its vision is not very
good. Miss Ladybird can get six red high-heeled shoes so that she is not
barefoot in the picture. Mr Butterfly can get a hat to stop
the wind from blowing his antennae around.

October

Safety advice: Be careful with electricity

Explain to your child the dangers of using electric appliances. Warn them that they are not allowed to plug in any electrical devices on their own. Tell them not to turn the light switch on or off if their hands are wet. They shouldn't touch cables on the floor either because they can be dangerous if damaged as they can give you an electric shock.

Susie Doll's birthday

Make a cake out of play dough. You can decorate it by painting it or sticking buttons or other small objects into it together. Sit Susie Doll and Teddy at the table.

Let's see how much of the cake each of them can get. Place the two halves in front of the two toys. When they are just about to start eating the cake, Rabbit and Ellie arrive. Put the cake halves back and divide the cake again. How many slices do we need to divide the cake into now? Cut it in four slices and put them in front of the toys.

When did each toy get more, when there were the two of them or when there were the four of them?

And if you wanted to have a bit too would Susie, Teddy and the others get more or less cake?

It is not important to mention the words 'half' and 'quarter'. What we want is that the child understands that each share will be less if we divide the whole into more slices, and each share will be bigger if we divide the whole into fewer slices.

A snake coiling up

Draw a coiling up snake on a sheet of paper with one movement.

But this is not a real snake because it doesn't have a body. The child's task is to draw the other side of the snake. Remind them that snakes are more or less the same width all along their body except their tail, which gets narrower and narrower towards the end.

When it's ready, draw some patterns on it and colour it in. If you are still up for drawing, make other, smaller snakes the same way, or even a big snake family.

You can even name the members of this family. Sneaky, Sissy and Rattler are good snake names.

Learn about maps

Any map of your country is good for this activity, but a less detailed map is better.

Sit down with your child and ask them to look at the map. For the first time it is enough to 'walk' along the borders of the country – ask your child to put a finger on the border line and slide it along. Draw the shape of the country in the air, too. Look at rivers and find lakes. Find the capital and your hometown. Any more information would be too much. Let the child talk and ask about the map.

Draw the map of an imaginary country together. Name this country and draw a national flag as well, for example, Fairyland, Storyland, The Ninja Empire. Use real map markings when you are drawing your map. Mark the borders with red and the rivers and lakes with blue. Make up names for towns and cities, too (there shouldn't be more than four), and mark them on the map based on the child's ideas.

Play with puzzles

Play with jigsaw puzzles, picture blocks or cut up pictures.

The aim here is to improve your child's attention span. It is a good idea to increase the number of pieces in the puzzle from time to time.

What is Helen doing? – Having dinner

Look for a list of names in a paper or the phone book. Pick a few different names. Focus on the first letter of the name and answer the question using the same letter: 'What is X doing?'

Help your child to understand this task by giving a few examples. It can be a difficult task, however easy it may seem.

'What is X doing?'

Sam – sleeping   James – joking
William – waterskiing   Tim – talking

November

Courtesy rule: Wipe your feet
Teach your child that whenever they enter a building, they should wipe their feet on the doormat. They should be taught to use the metal wire mats in front of shops and other public buildings. Explain to them why this is important.

Let's count with dominoes
Choose 10-15 dominoes from the set. Make the same number of small cards of the same size as the dominoes, and on them write down the numbers of the dots on each domino using the usual number figures.
Start playing the game by taking a domino and a card and try to find the card that matches the domino. Choose dominoes with lower numbers (0-5).
The dominoes and the cards should go in two separate rows.

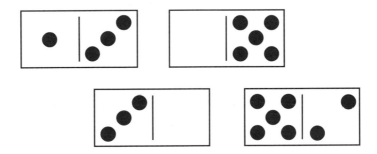

What could have happened?
This activity teaches the child that things happen in succession within the frame of time and space. Make up a short story. Prepare a drawing of the characters and objects that appear in the story, or alternatively, cut out pictures and make up a story that involves these characters and objects. Do not show the pictures to the child before telling the story. All you need to ask them is to listen to the characters and the objects in the story. (There shouldn't be more than five pictures.)
For example: 5cm x 5cm images of a hammer, a padlock and a key.
The story: 'One day a very strange thing happened to me. I wanted to go out to the garden but when I got to the door I noticed that there was a padlock on it. Next to the door there was my long lost hammer. I picked the hammer up but I didn't beat the padlock off with it, instead I went back to the house for the key.'

The child's task is to arrange the pictures in the right order, according to the objects' appearance in the story.
(Do not use a long story for this activity because the actions can distract the child from carrying out the task.)

 The animals are going for a drink
This is an excellent activity for developing dexterity and concentration. Draw or stick on pictures of four animals on a good size sheet.
Draw paths between the animals using a ruler. The paths shouldn't be wider than 0.5 cm / 1/5 inch. Draw a lake, where the animals can go to have a drink with a few paths leading there. The animals can keep visiting each other and going to the lake to drink some water. They are not allowed to step outside of or on the edge of the path or to touch a line. The movements of each animal should be marked with a different colour.
The game is over when the animals cannot pass without touching the lines. Keep in mind that the animals avoid going near any dangerous animals, so you could draw or place models of dangerous animals around the sheet.

 Let's learn a poem
Pick a funny poem that is not too long (2-3 verses). Repeat it a few times, then learn it by heart. You can also make an illustration for the poem. Then the drawing can decorate the wall in the child's bedroom for a while.

 When do you wear it?
A child of 5 or 6 years of age is expected to know a lot about the seasons. If their knowledge is weak you should draw a typical image of each season on four cards (for example, summer – the sun; autumn – a yellow leaf; winter – a snowman; spring – a blossoming branch).
You will list the following pieces of clothes and your child will pick out during which season they wear them.

knitted hat – winter
T-shirt – summer
jumper – spring, winter, autumn
tights – autumn, winter
sandals – summer
scarf – winter
jacket – autumn, spring
warm coat – winter
swimsuit – summer
boots – winter
shorts – summer
pyjamas – every night
short-sleeved blouse – summer
furry boots – winter
nice clothes – when celebrating something
sunglasses – summer
straw hat – summer
gloves – winter

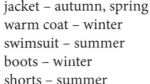

Courtesy rule: Give a present

Teach your child how to hand over a present nicely.

Make a small Christmas present for the teacher and the assistant teacher. Get the child to practise handing over the present, for example: 'This small present is for you. Happy Christmas.'

Let the child offer some food to the guests: 'Please have some, it's very tasty.' (They shouldn't just hold the food tray.)

Get familiar with the calendar

Months consist of weeks, and weeks consist of days. Learn the names of the months.

Write down the names of the months on a large sheet, one under the other. Ask your child to mark those months where something special happens (for example: a family member's birthday, Christmas, Easter, starting school, starting holidays, etc.). The child can make a drawing for each special month.

'The Best Month to Marry'

'Married in January's hoar and rime,
Widowed you'll be before your time.
Married in February's sleepy weather,
Life you'll tread in time together.
Married when March winds shrill and roar,
Your home will be on a distant shore.
Married beneath April's changing skies,
A chequered path before you lies.

Married when bees over May blossom flit,
Strangers around your board will sit.
Married in the month of roses-June,
Life will be one long honeymoon.
Married in July with flowers ablaze,
Bittersweet memories on after days.
Married in August's heat and drowse,
Lover and friend in your chosen spouse.
Married in September's golden glow,
Smooth and serene your life will go.

Married when leaves in October thin,
Toil and hardship for you gain.
Married in veils of November mist,
Fortune your wedding ring has kissed.
Married in days of December cheer,
Love's star shines brighter from year to year.'

Months Rhyme
30 days hath September,
April, June, and November.
All the rest have 31
but February's the shortest one.
With 28 days most of the time,
until Leap Year gives us 29.

Getting ready for Christmas
Prepare yourselves for Christmas by learning or practising poems and songs that can be recited or sung together under the tree.
For example: 'Jingle Bells'
                'Silent Night'
                'Hark the Herald Angels Sing'
                'Away in a Manger'
                'The Twelve Days of Christmas'
                'God Rest Ye Merry Gentlemen'
                'Joy To The World'

Riddles
Solving riddles is a great way to develop association skills, thinking in general and language skills.
1. Spinning my web day and night, running on it up and down. (spider)
2. I like eating leaves and grass, hiding my baby in my pouch. (kangaroo)
3. Up in the north I come and go, seal is my favourite food. (polar bear)
4. I give milk, meat and antlers; I'm the Eskimos' cow. (reindeer)
5. I like humming to your ears; I can sting you if you let me. (mosquito)
6. I am green and lazy, I hunt for prey in the Nile, say my name, I'm the... (crocodile)
7. I eat tree leaves for my snack because I have a long neck. (giraffe)
8. I'm a pie that rattles, and I steal everything that glitters. (magpie)
9. My nest is high up on the rocks, I like picking from the flocks. (eagle)
10. South pole is my beloved home, icy, snowy land I roam. (penguin)

Show your child how to draw a Christmas tree, a candle, a snowman, and other symmetrical shapes by drawing half of the picture yourself and letting the child draw the other half.

Mark the dividing line.

For example: You can make nice Christmas tree decorations by drawing these shapes on coloured paper that has been folded twice. You can then cut them out and glue the two shapes together.

 How can the sleigh slide down?
Try to choose many different paths.

January

Courtesy rule: Going to the cinema
Before the film starts talk about good manners in the cinema. It isn't fair to disturb the other viewers by making noise, talking, rattling with food wrappers and moving around while watching the film. You are not supposed to shout or clap in the cinema, either.

Looking at the map of Europe
Children at the age of five have probably heard people talking about travelling to Germany, England, The Netherlands or France. A child of this age cannot yet think in volumes as big as countries. Tell them that people who drew the map made very small on paper what's a huge area in reality.
Find your country on the map of Europe.
Name a few countries that your child may know already. Talk about what language the people in these countries speak. Say a few foreign words. If the child is learning a language search for those countries where people use the language the child's learning. Let them look at the map. Find national flags and make drawings of these flags.

Palm Puppets
Draw a figure onto your palm with a marker and act out a story that you make up together. (You can wash off the lines using a mixture of water and vinegar after playing.)

 Learn and practise the ordinal numbers
Read the following poem:

> 'Zero the hero,
> first the worst,
> second the best,
> third the one with the hairy chest,
> fourth the one with the golden gun,
> fifth the one with the cheetah's bum,
> sixth the one with a magazine,
> seventh goes to heaven,
> eighth the one that likes to read,
> ninth the one who needs to speed,
> tenth who runs lengths,
> eleventh smells a hyacinth,
> twelfth with wealth.'

Arrange some toys in a row and practise the ordinals: 'The car is the third one.'

 What is the food we eat made of and how is it made?
Tell your child about the ingredients and the making process of the various types of food and meals they enjoy eating.
Talk about these things while eating. 'Do you remember what I said to you about what the bread is made of? And do you remember how it is made?'
'I make your cocoa drink from cow's milk and the cocoa beans come from a tropical country.'

'Sunflower oil is made from sunflower seeds. Olive oil is made from crushed olives.'

'When they are making salami, they use meat pulp, salt and spices.'

Draw images of plants (wheat, potatoes, apples, etc.) and animals (pigs, cows, sheep) on cards and draw some food that is made from them. Mix the cards and ask your child to match them.

Riddles

1. My back is spiky, yet everyone loves me. (hedgehog)
2. I like jumping from tree to tree, I eat nuts and I eat seeds. (squirrel)
3. Flies and insects are what I eat, and I hate the birds' long beak. (frog)
4. I have no legs on the ground but I can still move around. (snake, worm, fish)
5. I can find what troubles the trees, I eat worms in big quantities. (woodpecker)
6. I'm digging day and night my underground home in the dark. (mole)
7. I sleep in a dark cave in winter, I eat berries and honey in summer. (bear)
8. Slowly, on my tummy I crawl, and I never leave my home. (snail)
9. I'm really bloodthirsty, my home is the deep blue sea. (shark)

February

Courtesy rule: We do not interrupt other people
Ask your child kindly but firmly not to talk when you are talking to somebody. Tell them that it is bad manners to interrupt, and that they should wait patiently until you finish your conversation if they want to say something. If it is urgent they need to say: 'Excuse me.'

Let's put together what we have
Place ten buttons in a little bowl and cover it with a cloth. Keep a bag of coloured counters at hand as well for marking the points you get to during the game.
Both of you should take out some of the buttons and act out the following short scene:
'Hello Peter.' 'How are you, Paul?' 'I would be great if I had 5 (6, 8) buttons. Let's put together what we have.'
After this both of you put the buttons from your hands in the centre of the table and arrange them according to the dot images (the images on a dice). If the person who guessed the number was right – and you have five (six, eight) buttons together on the table – they will get a counter. The winner is the one who makes more right guesses.
You should always use the dot images when counting the buttons.

Fashion long ago
Get a book with pictures of people dressed in clothes from a different century, and pictures of carriages, castles, etc. Look at these pictures and talk about people who lived before us. Tell your child that these people used to build different houses, used to wear different clothes and used to have different types of entertainment (for example, they played cards or told stories instead of watching television).
Long ago people didn't have electricity and they used candles for making light in the evenings. Every family made their own bread in an oven at home.
Tell your child about how your childhood is different from theirs.

Do you know the opposite?
We have covered the notion of opposite meanings in a couple of earlier activities. Now is the time to check your child's knowledge by doing a visual task. The child is supposed to provide their answer by drawing it.

	right answer:		right answer:
narrow road	wide road	tall	short
long	short	fat	thin
straight	crooked	lying	standing
forward	backward	light	heavy
round	angular	thin	thick
sharp	blunt	half circle	full circle

 Extend it

The game goes like this: you say a simple sentence and then your child puts in an extension, then it's your turn again to put in another extension, etc. The two of you keep extending the sentence as long as you can say it, using only one breath. (This task may not be easy for your child. You can help them by asking questions, such as, 'What is she writing?')

Kate's writing.

Kate's writing a letter.

Kate's writing a long letter.

Kate's writing a long letter for Peter.

Kate's writing a very long letter for Peter, etc.

 Whose head is it?

Draw 3-5 circles using a compass or by tracing around a coin. The task is to turn these circles into heads. They can be women, men with moustaches, cats, pigs, bears, elephants, old women with headscarves, little girls with ponytails, boys with caps, little mice, etc.

Courtesy rule: Look after nature

Draw your child's attention to blossoming trees, the fresh grass and the new leaves on the bushes. Ask them not to tear leaves and break branches off trees for no reason because they provide us with fresh, oxygen-filled air. (It's okay if the child doesn't understand what oxygen means. You can explain that it is clean fresh air that is good for us.)

How many more do you need?

Pick seven toy animals out of your collection. Pretend that all of them go to school. Place a napkin in front of each animal to put the animal's things on. Use small pieces of paper for books, matchsticks for pencils and crumbs for their lunch. You should give the child these bits and pieces but always give them less than needed. Keep asking your child: 'How many more do you need?'

Roll up the animals' things in the napkin, and tie these rolls on the animals' back with a piece of ribbon. Off they go to school.

Play music class (sing songs) and literature class (recite poems).

Interviewer wanted (or News on TV)

You can make a microphone out of the handle of a hairbrush or a plastic container and your child can pretend to be the interviewer and you pretend to be the interviewee. If the child is hesitant, you can give her ideas on what to talk about. For example: talk about domestic animals (cats and dogs), cars, shopping, household chores, gardens, going to school, etc. If the child is clever they can even read the news on TV.

The aim of this activity is to develop your child's interrogative and phrasing skills.

Mouse and elephant

Make it smaller and magnify it. Carrying out this visual task may be difficult for the child. You draw a middle-sized image of an object. The child has to draw a small image and a big image of the same object. One object goes to the mouse, and the other goes to the elephant. You can colour in the drawings then, using a different colour for each size.

Board games

Play with various board games. Board games are a great way to experience what it means to lose. Children need to go through this experience also, and get used to it and develop some techniques to cope with failure, which are essential, especially at school.

Discussing the Sun, the Moon, the planets and the Earth
You need three balls of various sizes for this session. Name the medium size ball Earth, the big ball Sun, and the small ball Moon. Model the movement of these planets. The Earth spins on its axis and it orbits around the Sun. The Sun spins around its axis, too. You can move the ball that represents the Earth around the ball that represents the Sun.

Imitate the Moon's circling motion around the Earth as well.

If the child has good memory skills, teach them the names of the planets starting with the Sun. This is the order of the planets: Mercury, Venus, Earth, Mars, Jupiter, Saturn, Uranus and Neptune.

Mnemonic device: A way to remember the order of the planets is to learn this poem: My Very Educated Mother Just Served Us Nachos.

(Note: The International Astronomical Union declared Pluto to be a 'dwarf planet' in August 2006. Pluto doesn't meet the requirements to be called a planet as it 'has not cleared the neighbourhood around its orbit'.)

Stress the importance of the Sun's warm rays without which there could not be life on Earth. There wouldn't be trees, bushes, flowers, animals and even people without the Sun.

Go outside at night and look up at the Moon and the stars in the sky.

 Free play
Go for an outing, run around, play ball outdoors.

Here is a family game: you need an instructor. If the instructor claps his or her hands once, everyone has to stop. If the instructor claps twice, everyone has to sit down, and if the instructor claps three times, everyone has to lie down. (This game can be played indoors as well.)

Courtesy rule: Be tidy

Teach your child how to make their bed. It is useful to make this chore part of their morning routine at this early stage. This will help your child to get used to independence and regularity.

Number parade

Cut a good length slip off a sheet of paper and draw small squares on it with the numbers from 1-6 or 1-12 in each of them.

Play with two buttons of different colours, one for you, and one for the child. You have to guess how many dots you will throw on the dice, and if your guess was correct, you get a point (e.g. a counter, a match stick or a coin).

You can use twelve numbers if your child likes adding up the dots on two dices. You should only play this way if the child is able to recognise the number straight away when they see the dice.

Play this game often.

(You can also get a point if you guessed the other player's number right.)

Living letters

Draw the letters of your child's name in approx. 2 cm size.

The task is to turn the letters into people by adding things to them in drawing. (Use block capitals.) Do not help your child with doing the drawing, but you can give them ideas about what to add to the letter.

Listen to your heartbeat

Place your child's hand on the heart so that they feel their own heartbeat on the left side of their chest.

Name the left side to your child. Their hand on the same side as the heart is their left hand, and their left leg is on this side, too. Their left eye and their left ear are on this side as well, etc.

Tell the child that the other side is called the right side.

Try the new knowledge by practising: stand in the centre of the room behind each other and ask your child to raise the hand on the side where they hear the sound that you name, for example: 'On which side do you hear the television? / the clock ticking? / the birds singing?'

You should always raise the hand and leg of the right side, too. This time your child should name the side. This activity should be played often, as it helps the child learn about directions, which is a basic piece of knowledge.

Clap and jump

Learn a poem or song lyrics by heart and clap to the beat.
It satisfies the child's great need to move around if they can jump along to the beat as well as clapping.
For example:

'London Bridge is falling down,
Falling down, falling down.
London Bridge is falling down,
My fair lady.

Build it up with iron bars,
Iron bars, iron bars,
Build it up with iron bars,
My fair lady.

Iron bars will bend and break,
Bend and break, bend and break,
Iron bars will bend and break,
My fair lady.

Build it up with gold and silver,
Gold and silver, gold and silver,
Build it up with gold and silver,
My fair lady.'

How can Doggy go home?

Try to find all possible paths using a different colour every time.
(If the child finds more than five ways you can rest assured, as their perseverance is excellent.)

Safety advice: Be safe on your bicycle

By now, your child might have learnt how to ride a bicycle. Point out the dangers of cycling to them. They should not only look after themselves but others, too. Agree on a safe route they can use where there is no great danger and where they are not a danger to anybody else. Remember, they need to always wear a helmet. Encourage them to ring their bicycle bell if they get too close to someone.

Get to know the car

Acquaint your child with the structure of the car. Both boys and girls are often interested in cars and vehicles. Most children will show an interest in pressing buttons and pulling levers. Make sure the car engine is off before you let your child examine the car. Show them the switches and the buttons and talk about the role of the speedometer, the indicator, the lights, the accelerator, the brake pedal, the hand brake, etc.

If the child seems interested, you can tell them about how the engine works too, but make sure it is at their level. It is enough for them to know that the petrol gets into the engine through some pipes where it burns, which generates a great force that can move the wheels around.

Warn the child that they mustn't touch anything on the dashboard unless you are present, but they are especially not allowed to touch the hand brake and the ignition key because playing with these can cause serious accidents.

Hand-made objects

You might have a few hand-made items in your home, such as ceramics, hand woven baskets or stitched tablecloths to show your child. Explain why these hand-made objects are valuable. If possible, try to make similar objects. Talk about the importance and joy in receiving a hand-made gift or card from a friend.

Play cards with numbers

Make small cards by writing a number on some of the cards and drawing the dot image on the rest of them. (Your child can help you prepare the cards.)

• Arrange the cards with the numbers in order and turn the other cards upside down. The child draws one card out of the dot image cards and puts it down next to the correct number card without counting the dots.

• The two of you share the cards: one of you has all the number cards, and the other has all the dot image cards. One of you takes a card from the other person, matches it with one of their cards and puts the pair down in the middle of the table. The dot images should be illustrated like this:

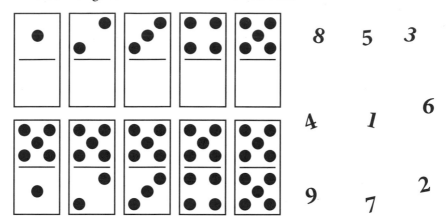

8   5   3

4   1   6

9   7   2

Pick the odd one out
Ask your child to explain why they chose that particular word.

Father	mother	neighbour
Car	bicycle	aeroplane
Plum	pie	grapes
Hard	cold	warm
Blue	smiley	red
Sailing boat	hang-glider plane	sea kayak
Giraffe	turkey	parrot
Swallow	whale	seagull
Shampoo	toothbrush	soap
Piano	violin	wooden spoon

The small naturalist
Collect leaves and flowers while walking. Group them according to their colour and their shape. When you get home put them between sheets of newspaper and place heavy books on them to make pressed flowers and leaves. After a few days, when they are dry, glue them onto a white sheet to make a montage (use clear glue). At the corner of the sheet mark which plants you used to make the picture. If you do not know the names of the plants, look them up in a book or on the internet.

Courtesy rule: Say no to bullying

Discuss the issue of bullying with your child. Explain that there are different types of bullying: physical, verbal and emotional. For instance, physical: pushing, shoving and hitting, etc. Verbal: name calling or saying nasty things. Emotional: excluding a child from a game. Many children have experienced and suffered from other children bullying them. Give your child some advice on this issue as well. Tell them that the best thing to do is not to respond to these remarks. However, sometimes it is inevitable that the child answers the bullies as if they do not respond, then the bully attacks them again and again. If your child finds the bully's behaviour very threatening, suggest that they ask for help from a grown-up they trust. The main thing here should be that the child has self confidence and strength in themselves and they shouldn't believe anyone who tries to belittle them. Advice in schools at the moment is: 'Say no, move away and tell someone'.

Let's play music

It is a good idea to visit a music shop – if you can.

Pick a time when you think that the shop assistants are not too busy and they have some time to answer your child's questions. If you cannot visit a shop look at a book with images of instruments in it and talk about the following ones: piano, violin, drum, cello, trumpet, flute, clarinet, recorder, etc. Mention that there are keyboard and string instruments. Try to categorise the above instruments together with your child (for example, *keyboards*: piano; *woodwind*: flute, clarinet, recorder; *brass*: trumpet; *percussion*: drums; *strings*: cello, violin.)

Talk about this topic two or three times. Listen to music played by an orchestra. Try and see a band play.

Life needs water

While walking near some water or during having a bath, talk about what would happen if water disappeared from the Earth. Try to make your child understand the importance of water. We quench our thirst and cook with it, we wash and bathe in it. Without water all the plants would die and most animals wouldn't have anything to eat and they would die. Without plants and animals people wouldn't be able to stay alive for long either because we would lack food. Tell your child about the water cycle: it falls down in the form of rain or snow, and this water gets collected in the mountains in small rivers first, then bigger rivers, and finally it flows into seas and oceans. From here it travels back into the air again and the wind blows it over villages, towns and fields. Water stored in clouds then starts falling down again re-starting the same cycle.

Colour while paying attention

Choose a page in a colouring book and ask your child to colour it. Point out that they should move the pencil in the same direction as the one they were using when starting the colouring, which ensures that the lines are neatly sitting next to each other. Help the child to pick out the best direction for drawing the pencil on the paper. The lines in the colouring should be short but they should emphasise the character of the drawing, for example, show them how to colour in the petals on a flower.

The child will probably start out like this. However, the veins on the petals call for a vertical colouring pattern. Practise producing various shades of colours (darker – lighter) as well.

Tearing words apart

Tear short words apart into letters. Help your child recognise certain letters in the words. Pronounce each letter inside the word you chose one after the other (for example, baby – b, a, b, y; car – c, a, r; milk, dog, hat, cat, bird, pen, sand, tree, leg, door).

How do the animals travel?

Assessment Sheets for children aged 5-6 years

As the final part of the book you can find 8 Assessment Sheets for 5- or 6-year-olds, which you can fill in together with your child. These sheets are designed to help you form a picture of your child's knowledge and assess which areas they are weaker at, so that you can concentrate on strengthening these particular areas by asking them to carry out activities that develop them.

Assessment Sheet 1

1. Please introduce yourself. Say…
   your name:_____
   where you were born, and your date of birth: _____
   your address: _____
   your father's name: _____
   your mother's maiden name: _____
   how many brothers or sisters you have: _____
   (Mark the answers with a + or a – sign.)

2. Continue colouring the pattern on the pearl necklace the same way as it was started. (Draw at least six more pearls on the string.)
   (R – red, Y – yellow, B – blue)

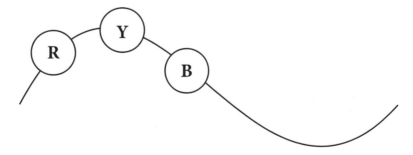

3. Anne and Peter meet in front of the supermarket. What can they talk about? Try to tell. *(To be able to put together five complete sentences is a good result – including greetings too.)*

4. Draw in the missing details of the following pictures.

(wings)

(hands)

(door, window, chimney)

(wheels, lights)

(ear, eye, arm)

5. Draw a slithering snake between the two lines. Make it touch the lines at the dots.

(The child should pay attention to the right shape of the wavy line.)

1. List the days of the week. ___ ___ ___ ___ ___ ___ ___
   Name the seasons. ___ ___ ___ ___

2. Draw in the missing body parts on this figure. *(Do not help by telling the child what to draw.)*

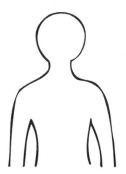

    eyes: _____   ears: _____
    hair: _____   mouth: _____
    hands: _____   legs: _____
    nose: _____

Draw on a moustache, glasses and a tie. *(Do not accept the drawings unless they are in the right place.)*

3. Draw in the right number of dots on the domino pieces. Say how many dots you had to draw.

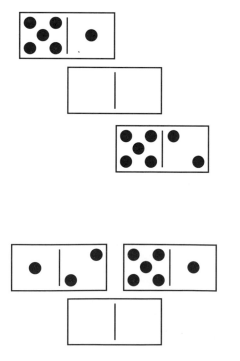

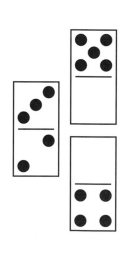

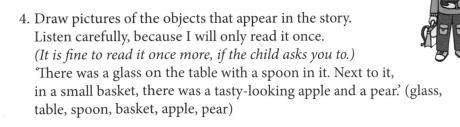

4. Draw pictures of the objects that appear in the story.
   Listen carefully, because I will only read it once.
   (It is fine to read it once more, if the child asks you to.)
   'There was a glass on the table with a spoon in it. Next to it,
   in a small basket, there was a tasty-looking apple and a pear.' (glass,
   table, spoon, basket, apple, pear)

   —— —— —— —— —— ——

5. Colour in the napkins using two different colours for each of them.
   They must look different from the other two. You can use blue, red,
   and yellow.

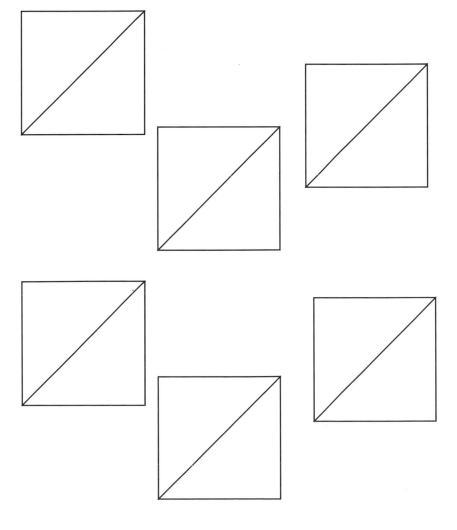

1. We'll play a game: you are the mummy (or daddy) and you want to enrol your child in school. I'm the school secretary who gives you information. Now, go out the door and come in again and pretend it is really happening. *(If the child can perform five steps, for example: knocking on the door, greeting, introducing oneself, wording his/her enquiry and saying 'thank you', it is a good result.)*

2. Make groups of the buttons in a few different ways.
   You decide how you are going to group them. Show which buttons belong to which group. Count how many buttons you have in each group. If the child is able to make at least three different groups, show all the buttons that belong to those groups and count them, that is a good result. They need further practice if they find less than three groups, miss more than two buttons, or make more than two mistakes in counting in each group.

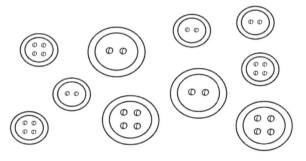

3. What colours would you use to colour the following pictures?
   Sun, cloud, grass, tree trunk, rose, snow, the night sky (yellow), (blue), (green), (brown), (red or orange), (white), (black).

4. Where do the following vehicles go?
   If you hear the name of a vehicle that goes on land – stamp your feet; if it goes on water or under water – pretend that you're swimming; if it goes in the air – pretend that you're flying.
   List of vehicles: car, helicopter, water-ski, ocean cruiser, underground, aeroplane, tram, surfboard, bus, motorbike.

5. Sing the 'Baa-Baa Black Sheep' song and clap the rhythm of the song, too.

Assessment Sheet 4

1. Name the building where you can find the following things or people.

lots of books	a library or a bookstore ___
pictures, paintings	an exhibition, a museum, a gallery ___
an organ (the instrument)	a church ___
thieves, robbers	a prison, a police station ___
doctors, dentists	a surgery, a hospital ___

   (You can ask about other concepts that the child has already heard of)

2. (Place a picture in front of the child in which something is happening.) 'Tell me about this picture. What is happening here?'
   It is great if the child can give a continuous talk. The child may need some practice in this area if they need to stop a lot.

3. What do the following animals eat?

rabbit (carrots, cabbages)	pig (swill, carrots, apples)
cat (mice, milk, meat)	fox (rabbits, field mice, hens)
stork (frogs, lizards)	mosquito (sucks blood)
horse (oats, hay, grass)	cow (grass)

4. Join the matching pairs of cards together.

5. Join the dots between the two lines drawing straight lines. Join a dot on the upper line with a dot on the bottom line, and join a dot on the bottom line with a dot on the upper line.

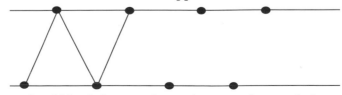

   (The lines should be definite and straight or nearly straight.)

1. What do the following people work at?

   Builder   builds houses

   dentist   cures, fills and pulls out bad teeth

   fireman   puts out fires

   animal breeder   feeds and cares for animals

   teacher   teaches children

   seamstress   makes clothes

   principal   is in charge of a school

   potter   makes pots and other objects

   shop assistant   serves customers, gives you the change

   librarian   helps you find or choose books

   Do not accept the answer unless the child describes the main responsibilities of each profession. They cannot give you just one word as an answer, for example, seamstress – sews.

2. We would like to buy three bunches of flowers at the market. Colour the flowers below using the colours listed for each bunch.
   Draw as many dots above each bunch as there are flowers are in it.
   (Use the domino arrangement for the dots.)
   You should only say the list of colours once.

2 red	1 red	3 blue
1 yellow	2 yellow	2 yellow
1 orange		

3. Draw a picture of what you see in front of you when you sing the Incy Wincy Spider song (a spider on the spout, rain clouds, the sun).

4. Look at these structures carefully and copy them.
   You should copy each of them on separate sheets of paper and ask the child to copy them next to your drawings.

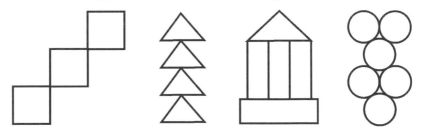

5. Peter and Paul moved into two different houses, in two different streets. Draw as many different paths between their houses as you can, and use a different colour for each route. How many paths did you draw?
   It is great if the child can find five or more different routes.

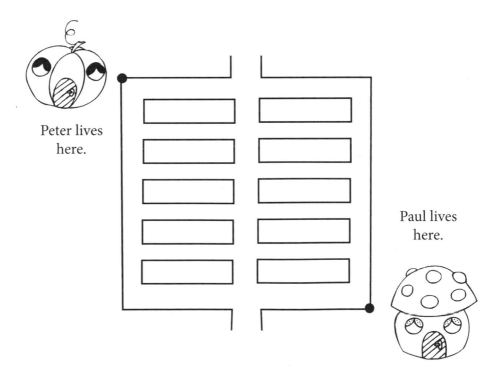

Peter lives here.

Paul lives here.

1. Think about what toiletry items you can find in the bathroom that you use. Tell me what you use each of them for. *(Ask the child to answer in complete sentences.)* (Soap, towel, shampoo, toothbrush, toothpaste, sponge.)

2. Pick the odd one out in each row and cross them out. Explain why they are different from the other cards.

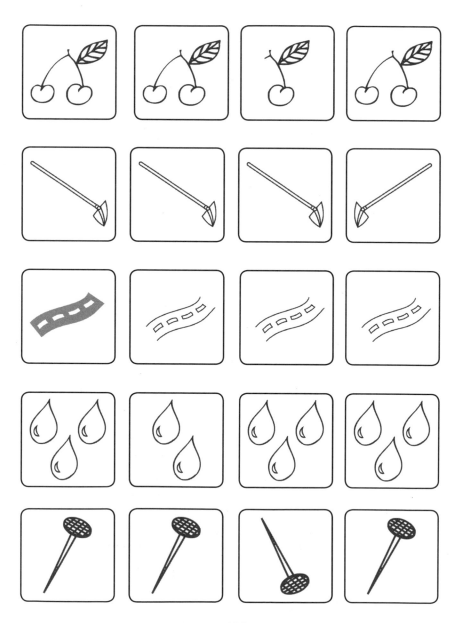

3. Place five buttons on the table.
'How many different ways could you distribute them between us (just two people)? Try to find all the ways.' (*If the child finds five solutions out of the six, it is a great result.*)

0-5
1-4
2-3
3-2
4-1
5-0

4. Sing 'Hickory Dickory' and clap the rhythm of the song.

5. Say the opposite word.

thin	(fat)
day	(night)
white	(black)
small	(big)
cold	(hot)
smart	(silly)
ugly	(beautiful)
good	(bad)
obedient	(disobedient)
brave	(cowardly)

1. Donald and Pluto are buying sweets in the shop. They put their sweets in the same basket. How many sweets will there be in the basket if each of them got the following amount of sweets?

Donald	Pluto	
1	1	/ 2 _____
2	2	/ 4 _____
2	3	/ 5 _____
3	4	/ 7 _____
3	2	/ 5 _____

(Let your child use small objects such as buttons to help them do the counting. Make them arrange the buttons according to the dot images.)

2. There is a sailing boat race on the lake. Three competitors are setting off.

Colour in the three sailing boats using different colours for each of them (red, yellow and blue). How many different results could there have been? In other words, who could have won? Don't forget: they may have sailed home at the same time.

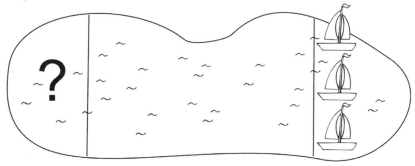

(Possibilities: red wins, yellow wins, blue wins, red and yellow win, yellow and blue win, red and blue win, all of them win)

3. Pick the odd one out.

You can accept your child's answer if they can give you a good explanation for their choice.

bicycle, motorbike, truck – (truck, because it has 4 wheels)

Judy, Kieran, Thomas – (Judy is a girl's name)

piano, stick, violin – (the stick is not a musical instrument)
school bag, shopping bag, beanbag – (the beanbag; we don't
put things in it, we sit on it)
trousers, shirt, jumper – (the trousers; we don't wear them on
our upper body, we put our legs through them, not our arms)

4. Copy this drawing three times.
   The child should pay attention to the decreasing circles, that they
   draw in the connecting line in the middle and the two triangles.

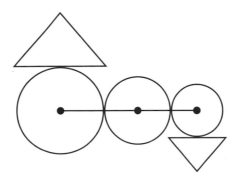

(You can check your child's perseverance with this task.)

5. Say a sentence using each of the following words.
   *(You should give an example to make sure the child understands the
   meaning of 'sentence'.)*
   The word: chair. The sentence: I'm sitting on the chair.
   parrot, fire, chicken leg, iron, mountain, bus, candle, spider web,
   teacher, rose.
   *(It is great if the child can say sentences that consist of 4 or more
   words.)*

1. Name three birds, three furry animals, and three animals without legs that can still move around. For example:

Birds	Furry animals	No legs
pigeon	fox	water snake
sparrow	dog	snake
owl	cat	fish
swallow	lion	dolphin
hen	tiger	whale
etc.	etc.	etc.

   (Any correct solution is acceptable, however being able to name 9 animals is good.)

2. Continue drawing the following rows.
   (The child should draw at least 6 pieces in each row.)

3. Draw a picture of what you hear.
   I will only read it once, so you will have to listen hard.
   (You can read it once more if the child asks you to.)
   'Lovely hot chocolate was steaming in the cup. Next to it was a bread roll, with a few bite marks on it. The fallen breadcrumbs were scattered all over the flowery napkin.'
   (a cup, a bread roll, breadcrumbs, flower patterns, a napkin)

4. Place 5 buttons or counters on the table arranged according to
   the dot images.
   Without touching them (if this is possible) the child should
   tell you how many sweets would remain on the table if you
   took away 1, 2, 3, 4, or 5 buttons/counters.
   (It is an acceptable result if the child needed to use the buttons/
   counters to give the correct answer. If the child didn't count with the
   buttons/counters and was able to give the correct answer, it is a great
   result.)

5. 'You are a ro-bot. You can on-ly speak slow-ly and break-ing up.
   Say the fol-low-ing sen-ten-ces in the ro-bot lan-guage.'
   I am a steel and iron robot.   I am a steel and i-ron ro-bot.
   I follow instructions.   I fol-low inst-ruc-tions.
   I don't like spinach.   I don't like spi-nach.
   (The child needs practice if they make more than two mistakes. One
   mistake is acceptable, and no mistake is a great result.)

Description of the child
at the end of the 6th year

Height: cm/inch

Weight: kg/lbs

Movements:

Some of their features:

Typical activities:

Level of speech development:

Favourite toys:

Favourite food:

Favourite books:

Some of their friends:

ALSO AVAILABLE FROM THIS PUBLISHER:

Kathy Dean

Aware PARENTS

LOTS TO SEE, LOTS TO DO, LOTS TO LEARN

An Activity Book
For Pre-school Children